A Record of the 58th Rifles F.F. in the Great War. 1914-1919

Gosling Press

Copyright © A. G. LIND
This edition Copyright Gosling Press 2023
All rights reserved.

ISBN 978-1-874351-24-5 (Hardback)
ISBN 978-1-874351-25-2 (Paperback)

Gosling Press

www.goslingpress.co.uk

Introduction

This book forms a fascinating insight into a single regiment of the Frontier Force's activities in the First World War. The focus allows it to consider their actions in more details than the more general history of the Frontier Force Rifles by Brigadier W. E. H. Condon. There was another history of the Regiment written by Colonel H. C. Wylly and published in 1933; this volume devoted a mere 21 pages to the regiment's participation in the Great War which was probably the reason for Colonel Lind to write this volume.

Vaughan's Rifles was originally raised in 1849 as the 5th Regiment of Punjab Infantry. Lord Kitchener's Indian Army reforms of 1903 meant that the Regiment's designation was changed to 58th, Vaughan's, Rifles (Frontier Force).

The Regiment was a mixed class regiment meaning that in 1914 the Regiment's class composition was three companies each of Pathans and Sikhs, and one company each of Dogras and Punjabi Muslims.

During the First World War the regiment was sent with Force A to France to serve with 21st Infantry Brigade, part of 7th Meerut Division. At the end of 1915 the Regiment was sent to Egypt where it initially served with 31st Indian Brigade and then in 1916 it was transferred to 20th Indian Brigade. It then served with the Egyptian Expeditionary force for the remainder of the war. Although one company was attached to PAMFORCE in East Africa during 1918.

This volume is of particular interest for its coverage of the story of the desertion of Jemadar Mir Mast and others of the regiment's Afridi Company. This is not the only incident involving certain classes of Sepoy. What is interesting is the Regiment's view of these incidents and the official views and responses which shines a light on some of the attitudes of the time. This is of particular interest when contrasted with the decisions about the 69th and 89th Punjabis during the Gallipoli Campaign.

A Record of the 58th Rifles F.F. in the Great War. 1914–1919

Colonel A. G. LIND, D.S.O.
(Commandant 1917–1926)

Edited by John Wilson

CONTENTS

	Introduction	i
I	France, 1914	1
II	France, 1915	24
III	Egypt And Sinai, 1916	51
IV	Palestine, 1917	63
V	Palestine, 1918	90
VI	Egypt, 1919	123

Appendices

A	Casualties	137
B	Honours and Awards	142
C	List of Units Providing Reinforcements	147
D	Recruits Enlisted	148
E	Extracts from Orders and Letters	149

Illustrations

I	Action near Givenchy 23 November 1914	14
II	La Quinque Rue 20/22 December 1914	19
III	Rue-du-Bois 9 May 1915	32
IV	Mauquissart (Battle of Loos) 25 Sept 1915	42
V	Jerusalem Pass 19 / 20 November 1917	79
VI	El Kefr 26 March – 6 April 1918	96
VII	Tabsor (Battle of Sharon) 19 Sept 1918	116

CHAPTER I
France 1914

In July 1914 the political situation in Europe was exceedingly acute, and on 4 August 1914 the long expected Great European War had commenced. On 12 August 1914, orders were received to mobilise for service overseas: the Battalion was to replace the 29th Punjabis in the 21st Brigade of the 7th (Meerut) Division.

Men on leave and furlough were immediately recalled, and reservists summoned to join the Colours. At this time the Battalion was being re-armed with the short M.L.E. rifle in replacement of the old long Lee-Enfield rifle which it had used for twelve years.

Lieutenant-Colonel W. E. Venour rejoined the Battalion and took over command on 15 August. Several officers being at home in England, on furlough, two officers were posted for duty vizt: Lieutenant J. McA. Craig, 57th Rifles F.F. Lieutenant R. A. Reilly, 31st Punjabis.

Captain A. A. Smith was detailed to command the Depot assisted by Lieutenant J. O. Nicolls. The Depot was to be formed at Chaman for the time being, with the prospect of being subsequently moved to Multan.

On 4 September 1914, the Battalion left Chaman in two trains which were united at Sibi, arrived at Karachi on the morning of 6 September, detrained quietly and moved into camp. Strength 12 British and 18 Indian officers, 809 other ranks including 2 sepoys detailed for the District Ammunition Column. The following British officers accompanied the Battalion – Lieutenant-Colonel

W. E. Venour (Commanding), Major A. G. Thomson, Captain A. G. Lind, Captain E. S. C. Willis, D.S.O., Captain J. D. M. Flood, Captain C. H. Elliot, Captain S. B. Pope, Captain R. A. Reilly (attached), Captain W. McM. Black (Adjutant), Lieutenant J. H. Milligan, Lieutenant J. McA. Craig (attached), Captain S. Gordon, I.M.S. Here it remained for twelve days while troops were concentrating and a large convoy of ships was in course of formation. Route marches and field exercises and practice in the new platoon drill were carried out, and the Battalion made the acquaintance of its Brigade Commander, Major-General F. MacBean C.B., and his staff and also of the 2nd Battalion the Black Watch, with which it was afterwards to be so closely associated: the other battalions of the 21st Brigade were the 2nd Battalion 8th Gurkhas and the 41st Dogras. The members of the Sind Club, Karachi, invited all military officers to become Honorary Members of their Club at this time: a privilege and a comfort, which will always be gratefully remembered.

On 16 September, the Battalion embarked. Headquarters and five companies, A-C, E and F, on the SS *Erinpura* – the other three companies on the SS *Aronda*. The ships remained in harbour until 20 September and then moved out to anchorage. On 21 September the convoy, escorted by HM Cruisers *Dartmouth* and *Hardinge* (Indian Marine), steamed for an unknown destination, which all hoped and believed would be France.

At about 2 p.m., on 24 September a large convoy of ships was sighted: this consisted of some 18 transports, which had come from Bombay and carried the rest of Indian Expeditionary Force A. At 3 p.m., the convoys met and formed into three columns of ships in line, escorted on all sides by cruisers of the Royal Navy. The convoy passed Aden at 10 p.m. on 27 September and arrived without incident at Suez on 2 October, entered the Canal the same evening and anchored at Port Said on 3 October.

At both Suez and Port Said, numerous German merchantmen, prizes of war, were seen. The days were chiefly spent in physical training and musketry exercises, but space was very limited, so little could be done. The weather, fortunately, was fine; as over 90 percent of the troops had never been at sea, nor in fact had they even seen the sea before. The remarks and conjectures were often amusing to listen to, especially as to how the way was found across the sea. One insisted that the Captain just kept the ship level with the horizon so could not go wrong: another after watching for some time the wake made by the propellers declared that the 'road' was plain to see. At Port Said Major C. Davidson-Houston rejoined from England and three days later Lieutenant L. Gaisford reported his arrival, having narrowly escaped being seized for some uncongenial duty.

The convoy steamed from Port Said at 5 p.m. on 6 October, and at dawn on 11 October arrived at Marseilles; the weather had been somewhat rough and the troops correspondingly done. Most of the vessels came into dock early on 12 October and began to disembark at once, this was soon done. Troops had to be re-armed at the docks with a new rifle, of which the barrel and bolt were specially designed to take the new cartridge, which carried a higher explosive and a new pointed bullet, giving a higher velocity and a lower trajectory. The remarks of the Afridis as they were ordered to throw their lately issued new rifle, worth at least 800 rupees in Tirah, on to a heap of other rifles and take a new one were worth hearing: they had never imagined there were so many rifles in the world.

At 5 p.m. on 12 October, the Battalion marched for its camp at La Valentine, some eight miles from Marseilles. It wended its way through streets lined ten deep with cheering inhabitants who offered a great welcome, and presented, indiscriminately, flowers, wine and tobacco to the men: invariably wine to the mohomadans, and tobacco to the Sikhs. After three weeks at sea and with soft feet, it was a weary march through the cobbled streets and suburbs of Marseilles and very late before transport arrived at the locality detailed for the Battalion camp. The weather fortunately was dry and tents were pitched shortly before rain commenced to fall heavily. The Battalion remained at La Valentine for six days which were chiefly occupied in sending large working parties to the docks at Marseilles to assist in unloading the various transports carrying stores.

On 18 October, orders were received to entrain at daybreak the next day. That evening the Battalion marched in to Marseilles in torrential rain and spent the night in one of the large hangars (huge sheds for the storage of merchandise) at the docks. The same day two cases of chicken-pox were reported in the Afridi Company, which had been contracted from the 41st Dogras on the SS *Aronda,* and in which unit there were a number of cases. Under medical advice, and much to its disgust, the Afridi Company under Captain A. G. Lind was ordered to remain behind, and had to march back to a segregation camp some miles out of Marseilles where it remained for a fortnight. The remainder of the Battalion left Marseilles at 10 a.m. on 19 October and arrived at Orléans on 21st and marched to camp at Cercotte. Here it remained until 26th and was fitted out with serge clothing and the new rack equipment: carrying their kit in pack was a new experience for Indian troops accustomed to being lightly equipped and dependent on mule and camel transport. The Battalion left Orléans on the night of 26 October and arrived at Berguette near Hazebrouck at midday on 28th.

It was now well in the war area and was soon appraised of that fact by the appearance of an enemy aeroplane, which dropped a bomb very near the train from which the Battalion was detraining. From Berguette the Battalion marched to billets in Robecg (seven miles). On 29 October the 21st Brigade marched to Gorre where the Battalion bivouacked in heavy rain. The Brigade was now within three miles of the trenches where continuous warfare had been going on for some weeks. Part of the Brigade was at once taken to relieve British troops in the trenches. The 58th Rifles was at this time in Brigade Reserve: the bivouac had become a morass in which the Battalion remained until 4 p.m. on 30 October, when orders were received to move up at once and reinforce the 2nd Battalion 8th Gurkhas who were suffering heavy casualties in trenches east of Festubert. On the way, the Battalion was switched off into a ploughed field and told to remain there in reserve pending orders. Information was received that the 2nd Battalion 8th Gurkhas had been shelled out of their trenches which had been occupied by the Germans, and that the trenches would be retaken by half a battalion each of the West Riding and the Bedfordshire Regiments, with the 58th Rifles and half a battalion, 107th Pioneers in reserve.

During this wait, the Battalion was introduced to its first experience of shellfire; a great many German shells falling into and around the field in which it was resting, but fortunately with very slight casualties.

Captain Black, Adjutant, went forward to report to the officer commanding Bedfordshire Regiment, who was commanding the retaking of the position. He was told that the Farm Y was held by troops wearing Gurkha uniform and talking Hindustani, but that our troops had been fired on from the Farm, and he was ordered to go up to the Farm and find out their nationality. No one knows exactly what Captain Black did, but very shortly after, he returned and reported that he had talked to the occupants of the Farm, and that they were Germans.

Soon after news was received that the attack had failed, and the 58th were to move forward and rush the lost trenches.

The night was pitch dark, rain was falling heavily and it was impossible to see more than a few yards to the front.

At 2.30 a.m., 31 October, the Battalion fell in and marched up the left hand branch of the 'Tuning-Fork' to carry out its first attack in the Great War.

No. I Company (Sikhs) under Captain Willis, with Captain Pope as Company Officer, was ordered to attack on the left across the open, and No. III Company (Sikhs and Dogras) under Major Davidson-Honston were to capture the Farm Y.

It was in more senses than one a matter of working in the dark: no one in the Battalion had ever seen the trenches or knew anything of the nature of the ground in front, or even how far off they were from their objective. Guides met Nos I and III Companies just past Festubert Church and led them along lines of approach across very intersected and waterlogged country.

The deploying position was estimated by sound and the intermittent light of German Very lights.

No. I Company lined up in a sunken watercourse, and could only cover the front to be attacked by extending the men finger-tip to finger-tip with the arms stretched out.

No. III Company was helped by the hedge along the Farm, and had no difficulty in getting into position.

No. II Company was in Battalion Reserve with Battalion Headquarters about 200 yards behind the attacking companies.

Captain Black, who had already been up to the Farm, took Major Davidson-Houston to reconnoitre through the gap in the Orchard hedge.

They crept slowly forward but were discovered by a Very light that went up, followed by rapid fire from the enemy.

Major Davidson-Houston flung himself flat on the ground, but Captain Black was too late, and fell shot through the heart.

So died a very gallant officer, who an hour or so before had performed a very fine feat of bravery, the details of which will never be known.

He had carried out his previous reconnaissance alone and in the pitch dark, over unknown country, the first time he had ever been under fire, and by his coolness and daring, he was instrumental in enabling No. III Company to capture the Farm with trifling loss.

Major Davidson-Houston now passed down word for the attack to be launched.

It was impossible to give a signal that would be heard all along the line. The only way to launch the attack was for the officers to advance and for each man to follow his neighbour as he saw him emerge from the sunken watercourse. And to the honour of both the companies, be it said, that not one single man failed to respond, when dereliction would have been impossible to detect.

The intervening country in front of No. I Company was a waterlogged field, full of immense mango-wurzels, over which it was impossible to advance faster than a walk, and the consequent tosses [of their feet – ed.], thought to be casualties but proved to be mango-wurzels, lent a touch of humour to a situation in which the ludicrous came as a welcome relief.

The trench was taken without difficulty, and a few tardy Germans quickly despatched with the bayonet. The two companies then set to work to gain touch inwards and on their flanks, a matter of much difficulty owing to the darkness, and to the mass of watercourses and would be trenches running in every direction, and to make preparations against a counter-attack which, however, never materialised.

At the first glimmer of light, Lieutenant-Colonel Venour, who had been restrained with much difficulty from leading the attack of the two companies, was seen striding across the open from the Battalion Headquarters to the front line.

He gained the trench successfully, and soon after looked out over the top, when he was thrown flat on his back in the mud by Havildar Lashkarai, an Afridi in charge of the signallers, who realised the danger. Colonel Venour's comments in the most virulent Pushtu, of which he was a past-master, left Lashkarai unmoved and ready to repeat the performance.

He immediately looked over again and unfortunately, Lashkarai was not quick enough. Colonel Venour fell back into his arms, into his arms, shot through the head by a German in a Gurkha head-dress at short range.

Thus in its first action in the Great War the Battalion lost both its Commanding Officer and its Adjutant.

Touch had been completely lost with Brigade headquarters, which were in Gorre. An aeroplane was therefore sent over to ascertain the situation in the front line. As it came over No. I Company's position, Captain Willis produced from his pocket a silk Union Jack, of the type that conjurers use, which shook out from a small ball to a flag of considerable dimensions.

This was waved at the aeroplane; the pilot leant out and waved his hand in answer, returning at once with the news, possibly the first instant in the Great War of cooperation of infantry and aircraft.

The enemy now commenced to shell the trenches in which the Battalion found itself: these trenches were little better than open ditches 9 to 15 feet wide and in places as much as 25 feet wide – badly sited and entirely without traverses. Shelling continued the whole day, accompanied by trench mortar bombs and rifle grenades from which the Battalion suffered heavily. Lieutenant Craig was mortally wounded and died in the trench. The trenches also were full of dead and wounded Gurkhas: certainly, the Battalion received its first baptism of fire in the Great War under the most adverse and depressing circumstances. It, however, hung on tenaciously to its attack position, ready to repel any for the whole of that day until midnight when it was relieved by the 41st Dogras. Two companies marched back to bivouac at Gorre the third company remaining as a reserve to the 41st Dogras in trenches. In this action, the Battalion had casualties 3 British officers and 5 Indian ranks killed, 4 Indian officers and 79 other ranks wounded: many severely.

The command of the Battalion was now taken over by Major Davidson-Houston and Lieutenant J. M. Milligan was appointed Adjutant. On 2 November, two companies moved up to Festubert and took over trenches from the Norfolk Regiment, one company remaining in reserve to the 41st Dogras: here the Punjabi Mohomadan platoons of No. I Company were heavily shelled and blown up by a mine: they retired to the support trench where they were reinforced by the other two (Yusufzai) platoons and remained in position. On 4 November the Battalion was concentrated at Gorre, marched to Festubert and was allotted a front of some 400 yards of trenches on the extreme left of what was the right section of the Meerut Division. As a matter of expediency and in view of the need of rapid reinforcement, one and a half companies occupied the advance trenches and one and a half companies rested in billets some 900 yards behind the line. Here the Battalion remained on constant duty until 24 November. It might be as well here to note briefly the disadvantages under which our Indian troops laboured and the difficulties with which, at this time, they had to contend. They had been thrown into action and trench warfare, with which they were quite unfamiliar, at a moment's notice: there was no chance of letting them in by easy stages to get accustomed to the conditions, and sending officers and parties up to work with seasoned troops in the line and learn from them the tricks of the game as was the case later on for the New Army battalions. All that was learned was the result of bitter experience.

They had been trained for hill and open warfare. They found themselves in trenches deep in mud and water, in underground warfare against an enemy well-provided with war material to which our men were quite unfamiliar.

The Germans had trench mortars, bombs, and rifle grenades, which found their way in to the narrowest trenches: iron loopholes, deadly sniper's rifles with telescopic sights, Very lights, periscopes and other aids to trench warfare with which our army was completely unprovided. The rank and file, with a pathetic faith in the superiority of the British *bandobast* above all other armies, could not understand why they could not have the same, and better, weapons of offence and why they had never been trained to use them. Our artillery, suffering from lack of ammunition and big guns, was unable to give that support so necessary for the morale of the infantry.

All this is very clearly detailed by General Sir James Willcocks, the Indian Corps Commander, in his book *With The Indians In France*[1]; and those who experienced the feelings of depression and anger at the failure of our nation to have prepared its armies for such a method of warfare, and saw their men suffering under

---

[1]Sir James Willcocks, *With The Indians In France* (London, Verdun Press 1920). (JW ed.)

every disadvantage and unable adequately to retaliate, know how bitter that experience was.

In its first action in the Great War, the Battalion showed great dash and steadiness and a laudable desire to close with and punish the enemy. That portion of the trench in which Lieutenant J. McA. Craig was mortally wounded was subjected to terrific shelling and that officer's last order was for his men to close in on either flank until the shelling was less severe; this was done but when Lieutenant Craig just before leaving, fell wounded, Subadar Abdul Ali remained with him and would not leave him until a party arrived with a stretcher. No. 3404 Naik Baidullah Khan also remained, bandaging and assisting wounded men. No. 1838 Havildar Roshan Khan (P.M.) lifted a live shell, which had fallen into the trench and threw it over the parapet before it exploded: another live shell fell into the trench, which he again seized, but it exploded in his hands killing him instantly. No. 1811 Havildar Karam Singh, although severely wounded in the chest, continued to command his section and showed most excellent spirit and example.

Jemadars Sohel Singh and Lal Singh and No. 2072 Havildar Diwana were all conspicuous by their coolness, cheerfulness and soldierly bearing: keeping their men well in hand throughout this very trying day. Lieutenant S. Gordon, I.M.S. was in the front line trench the whole day, moving along and dressing wounds: and when darkness fell, he personally superintended the evacuation of every wounded officer and man.

On 9 November, the Afridi Company, which had been detained at Marseilles on account of two cases of chicken-pox, arrived at Festubert: a most welcome and useful reinforcement.

Later on in the war, the fact of a man developing chicken-pox did not involve the segregation of the whole of his company: the medical authorities had to decide that it was unnecessary and a waste of manpower.

The trenches at Festubert in which the Battalion found itself were deep enough and narrow enough to be fairly safe: they were very wet and muddy and there was only one communication trench along 800 yards of front: such luxuries as dug-outs, inspection trenches, and trench boards were unknown at this time. All this made the nightly relief a long and very tedious affair. The support trenches were 300 yards in rear and unoccupied. Some 800 yards in rear were the reserve trenches, so waterlogged as to be almost untenable, but which could be held by the other half of the Battalion, in case of emergency. Behind these was half a battalion of French Territorial troops – old men: and behind them was the open country of France. One often wondered what would happen if the Germans had attacked heavily at this point.

The German trenches were 150 to 200 yards distant from our front line and they had in places sapped forward and made parallels, which brought them to within 80 to 30 yards of our front trench: in these sapheads, their snipers, provided with telescopic sighted rifles and behind iron loopholes, were continually on the lookout for a target. They blinded our wooden loopholes, laboriously erected during the night, and it was certain death for a man to show his head above the parapet for more than three seconds.

Our own Sappers and Miners and our Pioneers were being used as ordinary infantry to occupy trenches and the want of skilled labour and advice in sapping, countermining and using explosives was a severe handicap. These German sapheads were a source of great annoyance and worry and several local attacks were made on them on our own initiative. The most successful was carried out by a platoon of Afridis under Jemadar Said Razam: which entered the saphead, bayoneted some Germans who had remained there and brought back a number of arms and papers of value. During the whole of this time the fire of rifles or machine guns, rifle grenades or trench mortars, or shelling, was practically continuous and scarcely a day passed without several casualties occurring.

On 12 November Captains H. C. Baldwin and G. S. Bull, who had been on leave in England when the war broke out, and who had been employed in training the new armies, rejoined the Battalion.

At this time Field Marshal Earl Roberts, V.C., had been appointed Colonel-in-Chief of the Indian Expeditionary Force in France, was inspecting the troops in the neighbourhood and representatives of the Battalion were sent to meet him.

A few days afterwards, on 15 November, the news of his sudden death, from pneumonia contracted at the inspection, was announced – to the deep distress of all ranks. Earl Roberts was closely connected with the Punjab Frontier Force, which he had commanded from April to December 1878.

On the night of 15/16 November, a Yusufzai Naik, No. 2931 Jehandad, carried out a scouting exploit, which for coolness and initiative is worth recording. It was a misty night and he became separated from his companions and lost his direction. He was suddenly challenged in German, and found himself within a few yards of an enemy saphead. He replied "Musulman" and advanced quickly and by signs endeavoured to make it understood that he had deserted and wished to give himself up. He was taken into the trench where he succeeded in making the Germans understand that he was a deserter and that there were other men of his company who also wished to desert: and that he had come to arrange for this. He was taken back through and along a number of trenches, during which he made mental notes of all that he saw, and was finally brought to the German Battalion headquarters. Here the officers were evidently impressed and thought it worthwhile to try to obtain more deserters. After remaining near these headquarters all day, Jehandad was conducted at dusk to the same saphead and given to understand that at that place the Germans would expect him and his companions. He was then released and found his way back to his own company and was able to give much valuable information. Jehandad was specially promoted Havildar for this exploit by order of the Indian Army Corps Commander. He was unfortunately killed in action on 21 December 1914. On 19 November, the Commanding Officer received a message from the officer commanding the right sector that the Divisional Commander was greatly pleased with the activity shown by raiding parties and patrols of the Battalion.

On 23 November about 10 a.m., a report reached the trenches that the Germans had made an attack at dawn and had penetrated the trenches of the 34th Pioneers in the centre of the centre section of the Indian Corps front and were working their way along the trenches towards the right section.

About the same time, Lieutenant Reilly arrived with a small party from Battalion Headquarters carrying bombs and ammunition and reported that Captain Baldwin with two platoons had been ordered to occupy the support trench. Captain Lind who, with Captain Willis was in the front line trench, informed Lieutenant Reilly that, so far, he was inactive on his front and directed him to join Captain Baldwin in the support trench in case the latter required assistance. Almost directly after Lieutenant Reilly, with his party, had gone, a number of men of the 9th Bhopal Infantry, which unit was on our left, began to crowd up into our trench, saying that their unit had been driven out of their trenches by the enemy. An officer of the 9th Bhopal Infantry, Lieutenant G. Mortimer, came up and led his men back saying that he intended to hold the one and only communication trench that divided the sub-sectors held by the 9th Bhopal Infantry and the 58th Rifles. At this moment, Captain Willis was wounded in the face by a splinter from a bomb thrown from a German saphead, which had been brought to within 20 yards of our line during the previous night: and Captain Willis had to be evacuated to the right of the line held by the Black Watch. Captain Lind was thus left the only British officer on a front of some 400 yards. About noon, the enemy had penetrated the 9th Bhopal Infantry trench as far as the communication trench mentioned above and began to enfilade our section of trench with machine guns. (The difficulty of the situation can be seen from map I.) The whole formation of the front line trench at this point was very bad: it was bent back for some 200 yards to where the communications trench joined it and then continued obliquely backwards for some 100 yards: in the bend was a round house manned by machine guns of the 9th Bhopal Infantry, for the purpose of enfilading and protecting the right flank of their line. So far as is known these guns did not come into action and the section, including a British officer, were made prisoners.

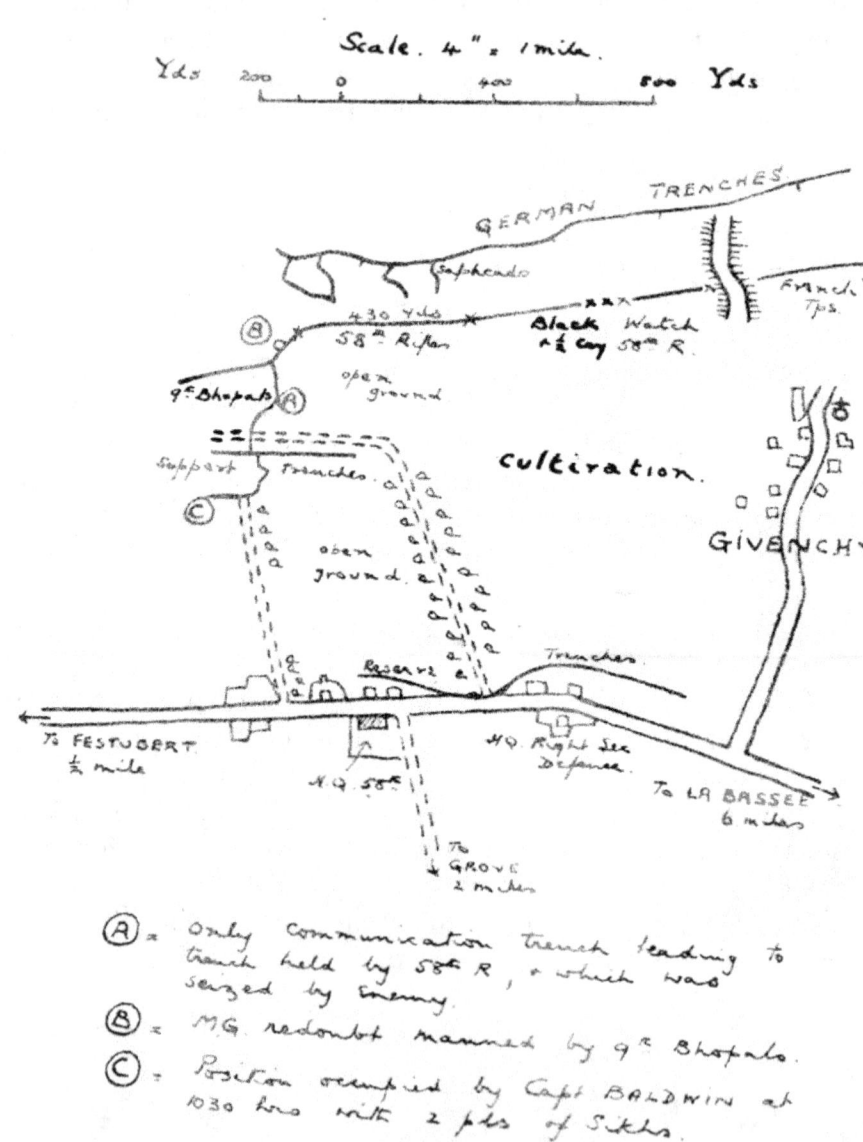

MAP I. Action near GIVENCHY. 23rd Nov. 1914.

(A) = Only communication trench leading to trench held by 58th R., & which was seized by enemy.
(B) = MG redoubt manned by 9th Bhopals.
(C) = Position occupied by Capt BALDWIN at 1030 hrs with 2 pls of Sikhs.

This trench, then, and the communication trench having fallen to the enemy, the line held by the 58th Rifles was open to enfilade fire from the left and left rear: casualties became numerous and it was evident that some 200 yards of trench must be evacuated. To protect his flank and rear Captain Lind ordered the left company (Sikhs) to get out and form a line to the left flank. This they did, but lost heavily in doing so and in the noise and confusion went too far and lost cohesion; eventually retiring in small groups on to the reserve trenches. The Afridi Company on the right, seeing the Sikh Company had moved out of their trench, thought that they were to form a supporting line to a flank and, with the exception of two platoons under Jemadar Mir Mast on the extreme right, vacated their trench and took up a position in rear, whence, later on, they joined in the counter-attack of the Battalion. Captain Lind, having seen the movement of the Sikh Company well in progress, returned to the Afridi Company, intending to barricade the trench, he found the Afridis gone. Having walked back through some sixty yards of empty trench he decided to follow the Afridis, but almost immediately on leaving the trench was severely wounded. The remaining two platoons of Afridis stayed in their trench and were shortly afterwards joined by Captain G. S. Bull who had been sent from Battalion Headquarters to replace Captain Willis (wounded) and who joined the line by following the only other available communication trench, which led to the line held by the Black Watch on our right. Captain Bull at once barricaded the trench and held the enemy in check with bombs and rifle fire until the counter-attack took place some three hours later at 4.30 p.m.

Meantime arrangements had been made for a general counter-attack at 4.30 p.m. This was carried out after and under a most effective artillery of the Battalion bombardment. The rest supported by two platoons of the Black Watch moved straight on to the lost trenches carrying all before them, and regained their trenches with few casualties, taking a number of German prisoners. Our total casualties, however, were very heavy – these being mostly in the Sikh Company.

Captain Baldwin's party in the support trenches held the enemy in his front in check all day and joined in the counter-attack.

Both Captain Baldwin and Lieutenant Reilly were killed. Lieutenant L. Gaisford was killed in the counter-attack. Jemadar Wazir Singh and 42 other ranks were killed, 11 others were missing and all probably killed. Captains Lind and Willis, Subadar Gujar Singh, and 61 other ranks were wounded.

The following officers and men were specially brought to notice for gallantry in this action.

Captain G. S. Bull, who with Jemadar Mir Mast and No. 3572 Havildar Saidak (Afridis), were successful in preventing the enemy from penetrating further along our line after the Sikh Company had fallen back and half the Afridi Company had taken up a position in rear under a misapprehension.

Captain Bull was awarded the Military Cross and Jemadar Mir Mast and Havildar Saidak the Indian Distinguished Service Medal.

Lieutenant S. Gordon, I.M.S. spent the whole night in attending to and searching for wounded. He returned again the next night with Captain Bull and Lieutenant Milligan and discovered several more wounded, returning to billets at 5 a.m. on 25 November. The fact that only 11 men, amongst such heavy casualties, were unaccounted for attests to the excellence of his work and that of his stretcher bearers.

Captain Baldwin held on to a very exposed position all day from which troops from units of the left section were constantly falling back. He was killed leading his men forward in the counter-attack in the evening. No. 1869 Havildar Indar Singh, who was with Captain Baldwin throughout, continued to lead this party with skill and determination, after Captain Baldwin had fallen. He was promoted Jemadar and awarded the Military Cross.

No. 3212 Havildar Lashkarai (Afridi), the Signalling Havildar, had previously, and especially on this occasion, done splendid work in keeping his telephone in working order, and in taking repair parties out to mend lines which were being cut by heavy shell fire.

Jemadar Hamid Khan (Yusufzai), Jemadar Raj Talab and No. 3297 Lance-Naik Sher Gul (P.M.s) were also conspicuous in leadership. The last named cleared a sap head which the enemy had cut right into our line during the day, killed two Germans and picquetted the sap single-handed until help arrived. Gul Sher was killed in action on 21 December 1914.

The Battalion was relieved just before dawn on 21 November by detachments of Indian cavalry, and marched back to Gorre: and next day moved to Essars where it remained in billets until 3 December. On 1 December a party of 2 Indian officers and 100 other ranks, under command of Captain G. S. Bull, M.C., marched to Locon where, with other units of the Brigade, they were inspected by His Majesty the King who was accompanied by H.R.H. the Prince of Wales.

On 3 December, the Battalion marched to Festubert and the same night two companies relieved the 20th Deccan Horse in the centre of the right section of the front line. The Battalion held this front until 11 December when it was relieved by the 125th (Napier's) Rifles. During this period, the following reinforcements were received: Captain A. A. Smith from the Battalion Depot in India, and Captain M. A. Bell, 54th Sikhs F.F. arrived on 6 December. Captain F.F. Hodgson, 84th Punjabis, Captain P. Hore, 52nd Sikhs F.F. and Captain D. G. Robinson, 46th Punjabis, arrived on 12 December.

On 9 December, a reinforcement of 2 Indian officers and 204 other ranks of the 91st Punjabis arrived and were posted to the Battalion. On the same date Captain C. H. Eliot, was wounded somewhat severely when returning from trench duty, by a stray bullet.

On the night of 11/12 December the Battalion marched to billets in Vendin, on 14th to Lehamel, on 17th to Oblingheim, on 18th back to Lehamel and on 19th to the Rue de l'Epinette. The weather was cold and rainy and all this marching and counter-marching most trying.

On 20 December, another battle had begun. At 10.45 a.m. on that date, the Battalion was ordered to move to a position half a mile west of La Quinque Rue to support the Seaforth Highlanders and the 2nd Gurkha Rifles. For about 40 hours from now the Battalion was engaged in filling the gap between the left of the Seaforth Highlanders and the right of the 2nd Gurkha Rifles – caused by the latter battalion having been bombed and shelled out of its trenches. Very heavy fighting ensued, but the Battalion more than held its own and succeeded in regaining portions of the lost trenches and preventing a breakthrough by the enemy. Most conspicuous and excellent work was done by No. IV Company (Afridis) and by the Yusufzai platoons of No. II Company: also by that portion of the Punjabi Mohomadan platoons of No. II Company, which came into contact with the enemy. The Battalion machine guns also distinguished themselves greatly in this action. Extracts from the Commanding Officer's report on this action, will explain the events as they occurred (see map II).

> 12.30, 20 December – No. IV Company under Captain Bull pushed up road past the Brewery: here they met fugitives of the 2nd Gurkhas. Noticing the situation was serious Captain Bull pushed on, seized some cottages D, 100 yards beyond the Brewery and held up the German advance which was pouring down the support trench marked A,
>
> 2.30 p.m., 20 December – No. III Company, Captain Smith, sent to point B to dig in.
>
> 3 p.m., 20 December– Half No. II Company under Captain Bell sent to communication trench at 'C' to check German advance. Captain Bell was killed at about 1p.m. Captain Hodgson sent to replace him.

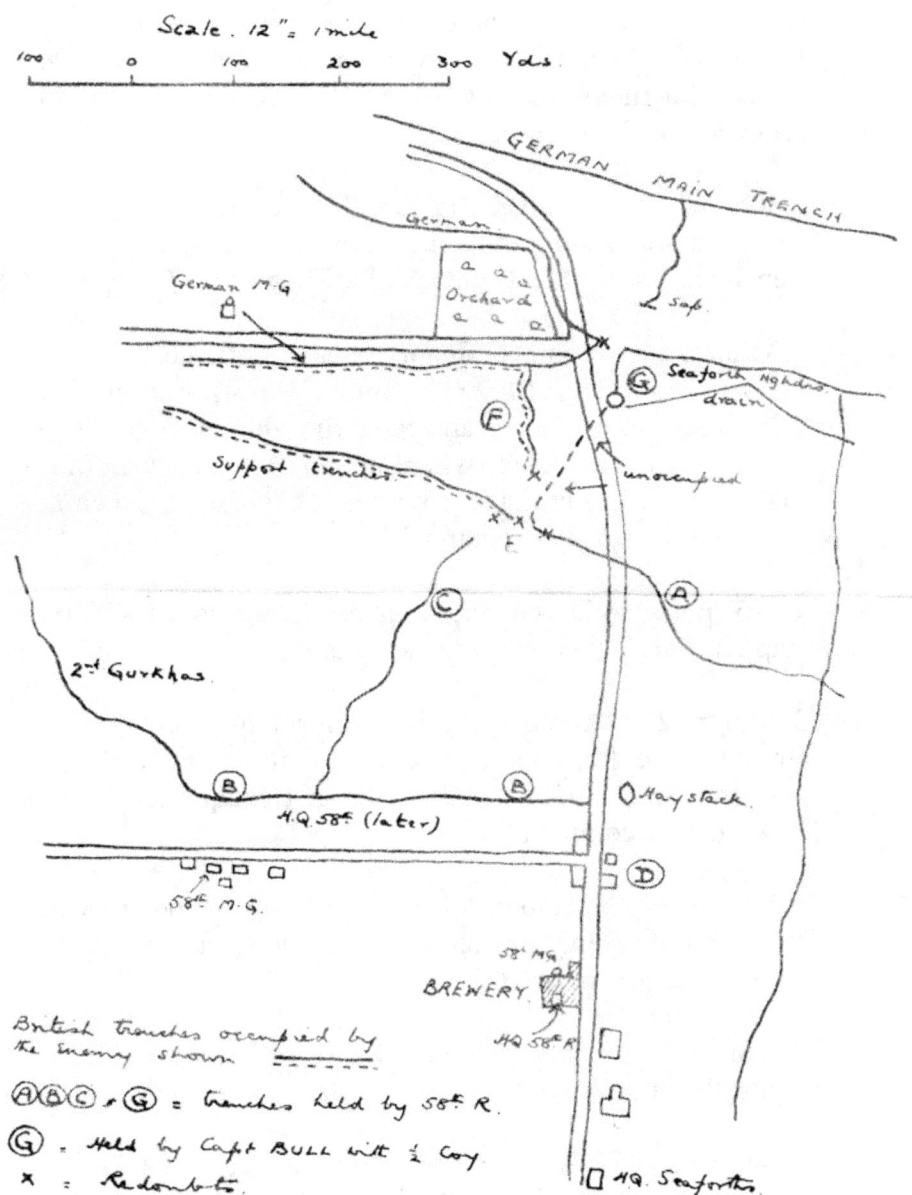

5 p.m. 20 December, half No. II Company (Yusufzai) under Major Thomson sent to reinforce No. IV Company (Captain Bull) which had advanced and was clearing the support and communication trenches on the left of the Seaforths. They had by now cleared some 250 to 300 yards with intensive bombing (NB these they held until relieved on 22 December).

7.30 a.m. 21 December, Captain Hodgson led a charge of some 16 men across the line marked E to the support trench and joined hands with Major Thomson.

8.35 a.m. 21 December, Enemy opened enfilade fire with machine guns on Major Thomson's left, killing and wounding some 13 men and rendering this portion of the trench untenable: touch with Captain Hodgson was thus lost, and enemy, pressing down communication trench at F, forced him to retire again to C.

12.15 p.m. 21 December, Captain Hodgson at C and Captain Smith at B reported they were holding their own.

3.50 p.m. 21 December, received information that the 2nd Brigade would counter-attack at dusk: ordered to cooperate with fire: moved Battalion Headquarters to B. Saw officers commanding.

6.30 p.m. 21 December, left of North Lancs, and right of Northampton Battalions and told them to keep touch with communication trench C.

9 p.m. 21 December, A North Lancs orderly came in to report the attack had been successful.

12.40 a.m. 22 December, received message that "if no unsatisfactory developments" to withdraw Battalion to Richebourg St Vaaste.

5.30 a.m. 22 December, having satisfied myself that the support trench (see sketch) was strongly held by the North Lancs Battalion, ordered companies at B and C to withdraw to Brewery and informed companies under Major Thomson they would be relieved by Royal Sussex Battalion probably about 8 a.m.

7 a.m. 22 December, situation being apparently normal, despatched two and a half companies at intervals to Rue de l'Epinette: and took Battalion Headquarters after the last half company.

3 p.m. 22 December, Captain Bull with remaining details of the Battalion arrived at Richebourg. The arduous nature of the fighting under Major Thomson and Captain Bull, Captain Hodgson and Captain Hore may be judged by the fact that from 36 to 40 hours they were within hand-bombing distance of the enemy on three separate lines of trench: and that they threw over 150 bombs and gained ground at all points. Major Thomson, Captain Bull and Captain Hodgson and Captain Pope all received bullets. It has been very difficult to select names, as in a long sustained effort of this nature, when men are every moment risking their lives; many acts of bravery are done which pass unnoticed.

The casualties in this action were, killed, 1 British officer Captain M. A. B. Bell, 54th Sikhs F.F., 1 Indian officer, Jemadar Mardan Ali (P.M.) 24 other ranks: and 32 other ranks wounded. Amongst the killed were No. 2931 Havildar Jehan Dad (Yusufzai) and No. 3297 Lance-Naik Sher Gul (P.M.) who had repeatedly distinguished themselves in action.

The following officers and men were specially brought to notice: Major A. G. Thomson, who commanded our men on the left flank of the Seaforths throughout the fighting and drove the enemy back some 300 yards and held the trench against all efforts to dislodge him. He and his men were constantly exposed to a close fire of bombs and rifles for some forty hours: his determination effectually checked the enemy and prevented the left flank of the Seaforths being surrounded.

Captain G. S. Bull, M.C., who commanded the company first pushed forward to the Brewery and by his prompt action and grasp of the situation checked the enemy who were rapidly pressing forward and who would have seized the Brewery in a few minutes. Later on, he was most active in assisting Major Thomson, and though knocked down and stunned by the explosion of a shell continued at his post.

Captain F. F. Hodgson, 84th Punjabis (attached) who commanded in the communication trench leading from the support to the reserve trenches, a post of extreme importance and danger, as the enemy held both sides of the support trench where this communication trench ran into it. Observing a retrograde movement of the enemy, he immediately led a charge with some 16 men, and although he lost 5 of his number at once, he gained a footing in the support trench, and held it until driven out by machine gun fire.

Jemadar Harchand Singh, who, with his machine gun detachment Nos.2658 Naik Lal Singh, 2818 Sepoys Ghulam Mohammad (P.M.), 3319 Atma Singh, 2842 Mangtu, and 3074 Sheraza Khan, (Afridi) supported the counter-attack on 21 December – firing over 3,000 rounds and continuing in action although the enemy artillery had located his position and were putting shell after shell about the house he was in, shattering rooms on either side of him.

No. 2834 Lance-Naik Sher Khan (P.M.) was throughout in the most exposed position in trench C continually bombing, and being bombed by, the enemy. He pointed out to Captain Hodgson, the retrograde movement of the enemy and with him led the charge on the support trench.

No. 3572 Havildar Saidak, 3032 Lance-Naik Lal Badshah, 2634 Naik Zerghun Shah, and 3097 Sepoy Azam Khan (all Afridis) distinguished themselves by most skilful and daring bomb throwing, taking on the enemy wherever the situation demanded.

These men were exposed to enemy bombing continually for some 36 hours.

No. 2763 Havildar Ajun Khan, who commanded his section on the extreme left, and nearest to the enemy, with great skill, repulsed every attempt of the enemy to make ground. The Seaforth Highlanders were very grateful for the support and protection afforded to their left flank and rear and spoke highly of the élan and initiative shown by the Battalion. The men were in high spirits after this action and it was here that they nicknamed their bombs *Alemand ka ration*.

CHAPTER II
France, 1915

The Battalion remained in reserve at Richebourg St Vaast until 27 December when it marched by stages to Fontaines-Les-Hermans, arriving on 29 December, and here it remained enjoying a well-earned rest until 25 January 1915. During this period the following officers joined the Battalion:
Captain J. Y. Tancred, 19th Punjabis, on 2.1.15
Captain E. Grose, 16th Rajputs, on 8.1.15
Lieutenant S. A. MacMillan, I.A.R.O., on l3.1.15
Captain C. G. V. M. Wardell, 21st Punjabis on 21.1.15

On 25 January 1915, Subadar-Major Mir Alam Khan, Sirdar Babadur, was sent to Marseilles en route to India to take over the duties of Subadar-Major of the Depot and assistant to the officer commanding the Depot. The latter at this time, a somewhat junior officer and the excellent work put in later on by Subadar-Major Mir Alam Khan, thoroughly justified this order, which Lieutenant-Colonel Davidson-Houston had reluctantly given.

On 25 January the Battalion marched to La Pierrière where it remained in billets until 31 January, on which date it marched to Vendin-Les-Bethune and thence to Les Facons where Headquarters and half the Battalion remained in billets; the other half Battalion taking over trenches east of the Rue-du-Bois. The weather was very wet, communication trenches full of water and unusable: the ground was so waterlogged that breastworks had to be erected and occupied in place of trenches, giving an excellent mark for enemy artillery. During this period 2 men were killed and 7 wounded.

Subadar Phuman Singh was severely wounded on 8 February and died at Boulogne on 13 February. His work since the Battalion first came consistently into action had been good: always cool under fire and active and energetic in the trenches, freely exposing himself to danger when necessary and setting a fine example to all ranks. He was a fine athlete in his day; a great wrestler, runner and jumper and a man of magnificent proportions,

The Battalion was relieved by the 4th Gurkha Rifles on 9 February and went into billets in Vielle Chapelle. On 12 February a portion of a company of the 82nd Punjabis consisting of 3 Indian officers and 97 other ranks under command of Major J. W. Milne joined as a reinforcement: the remainder of the company, 1 Indian officer and 107 other ranks had been segregated at Marseilles on account of mumps. That portion which joined the Battalion also contracted mumps and had to be segregated on arrival.

On 12 February the Bareilly Brigade marched to Le-Petit-Pacgaut – south of Merville where the Battalion remained until 23 February and enjoyed a period of very necessary bathing and washing at the baths erected in the local breweries.

During this period a number of Decorations and Mentions in Despatches were announced as having been awarded to officers and men of the Battalion for gallant and distinguished service during the past three months. These included: one Distinguished Service Order, two Military Crosses, eight Indian Orders of Merit of the 2nd Class, one Order of British India of the 2nd Class, twelve Indian Distinguished Service Medals, and eleven Mentions in Despatches (the names of the recipients are in Appendix B).

On 24 February the Battalion marched to Vielle Chapelle and remained there in billets until 2 March: when in conjunction with the Black Watch it took over trenches in B sub-section from the

Cinder Track to the Orchard. At this time two companies of the Battalion were attached to the Black Watch, and two companies of that Battalion to the 58th. The former were in occupation of C sub-section.

It was now that there occurred in the Afridi Company an event that will never be forgotten nor forgiven in this Battalion. At 1 a.m. on 8 March, Captain Tancred, commanding the Afridi Company, when visiting his picquets found that No. V picquet, garrisoned by 1 non-commissioned officer and 6 men, all Afridis, was empty. There was no sign of a struggle and no disturbance had been heard or reported: indeed, the night was particularly calm, and there was very little rifle fire. As soon as possible this picquet was reoccupied by a non-commissioned officer and 12 other Afridis under Jemadar Mir Mast, I.D.S.M., who had distinguished himself greatly in every action hitherto and had at all times shown excellent example and reliability. The non-commissioned officer with him was Havildar Guli Jan, of whom more will be said later on.

Further precautions were taken: 40 rifles of the Afridi Company in Section Reserve being replaced by men of the Black Watch and Dogras of No. I Company. The same evening, 3 March, about 6 p.m. a visiting patrol consisting of 2 men of No. IV Company (Afridis) was sent towards No. V picquet. As these had not returned by 7.30 p.m. a party was sent out to investigate. No. V picquet was again found empty. There was now little doubt that both these parties had deserted their picquet and gone over to the enemy: and the only reason that could be attributed was that the movement was instigated by Havildar Guli Jan, whose *amour propre* had been offended by his not being promoted to a vacant Jemadari. This man had suffered from swollen head and general irresponsibility ever since he had been specially promoted Lance-Naik for some act of initiative in pre-war days. The Commanding Officer had interviewed him a few days before on the subject of his non-promotion to Jemadar and had explained the reasons: and Guli Jan had promised to show better example, and if given the chance to prove he had plenty of pluck. Amongst the men of the first picquet which had deserted were two particular friends of Guli Jan and he had at once volunteered to go over to the

German lines, as had (inadvertently) been done by Havildar Jehandad, in November 1914 and endeavour to bring them back. This, of course, was not permitted. But the officer commanding the Afridi Company thought he might effect something under the eye of the supposedly thoroughly reliable Jemadar Mir Mast, and so put him in the picquet. It was a most unfortunate decision. The discovery of this desertion was a terrible blow, especially the treachery of Jemadar Mir Mast, whose courage, devotion to duty and reliability had hitherto been unquestioned.

Under orders from the Brigade Commander, the remainder of the Afridi Company was disarmed and marched back to Locon under a guard of the Seaforth Highlanders; the left flank of which battalion they had so gallantly protected in the fighting of 20–22 December 1914. The remainder of the Battalion was relieved by the 4th Suffolk Battalion, and went into Brigade Reserve.

Later on, the rest of the Afridi Company having expressed their disgust at the disloyalty of the deserters and their intention of continuing to serve loyally if given the chance to wipe out the disgrace attaching to them, and after certain relations and possible sympathisers with the deserters had been removed, and sent to serve with a Cooly Corps in Egypt, Army headquarters permitted them to be re-armed and re-instated in the Battalion. Of these deserters, nine were captured by Russian Cossacks in the spring of 1917 in company with a party of Germans and Turks proceeding to Afghanistan. They were brought to Egypt for trial and given 14 years transportation – a very inadequate sentence. Jemadar Mir Mast returned to Tirah, and endeavoured to raise an Afridi Army to fight for the Turks: he received little encouragement, however, and died of influenza in the virulent epidemic of 1919. Guli Jan remained in Germany for some time after the Armistice in 1918. He was reported as keeping a small tobacconist shop in Berlin and supplementing his income by keeping there ladies of easy virtue. He returned to Tirah with a German wife in 1921.

The remainder of the Afridi Company rejoined the Battalion about the middle of April 1915, under instructions from the Corps Commander General Sir James Wilcocks.

On 7 March, two companies of the Battalion with two companies of the Black Watch again relieved the 4th Suffolks in trenches: the third company being attached to the Black Watch.

On 10 March 1913 the Battle of Neuve Chapelle commenced and continued until 13 March. So far as the Indian Corps was concerned it was eminently successful. The role of the Bareilly Brigade was merely to hold its front and cooperate with fire and observation. Throughout, our trenches were shelled more or less heavily by the enemy and on the 12th he tried a half hearted attack in misty weather on our front: this was easily repulsed and 70 enemy made prisoner. On 13 March, the Battalion was relieved by the 129th Baluchis and marched to billets in Paradis. Our losses in this action were Captain A. A. Smith, Captain E. Grose, and Captain C. V. M. Wardell, all wounded: 11 other ranks killed and 1 Indian officer and 24 other ranks wounded.

Although the Battalion was not called upon to take a prominent part in the fighting at Neuve Chapelle it underwent considerable strain and constant shelling for the three and half days the battle continued. Amongst many individual combined acts of gallantry reported, the following are selected.

Nos 3163 Gurmukh Singh, 3319 Atma Singh, 2790 Waris Khan, 2974 Diwan Ali, 2018 Wilayat Khan, all stretcher bearers, showed special devotion to duty and disregard of danger in bringing in at great personal risk many wounded of our own and other regiments both by day and by night. Jemadar Mohammad Arabi, 2198 Havildar Fazal Dad, 3863 Sepoys Wilayat Khan, and 3883 Shah Sowar (P.M.s) were carrying material to repair picquet when their attention was drawn to a wounded man whose cries for help had attracted a heavy fire on himself and on the picquet from the enemy about 100 yards away. Led by the Jemadar they went over the parapet and carried the wounded man into the Orchard trench some 80 yards, all the time under heavy fire.

No. 3083 Naik Zar Baz and No. 3882 Sepoy Gujar (Yusufzai) were, amongst others, on guard over a house containing bombs and ammunition. The house was struck several times by shells, and the rest of the guard were killed or wounded but these men stuck to their post throughout. Naik Zar Baz was wounded early in the war but had returned to duty and had lately distinguished himself by carrying out a daring and important piece of scouting in company with some men of the Black Watch.

No. 2460 Signalling Naik Mastana (Dogra) constantly out by day and night during the battle repairing the telephone wires under shell fire and maintaining communication with Headquarters.

Subadar Sohel Singh, I.O.M., 2072 Havildar Diwana (Dogra) 2212 Havildar Punjab Singh, 2651 Havildar Natha Singh, 3850 Sepoy Jawand Singh, and 3896 Sepoy Santa Singh, on 12 March showed conspicuous gallantry in carrying bombs and ammunition to Port Arthur redoubt. The working party of another unit had refused to go on under the heavy fire, and had put down their loads. Led by Subadar Sohel Singh, these non-commissioned officers and men made three journeys with the loads, getting them all in to the redoubt where they were urgently required.

Subadar Sohel Singh was awarded the 1st Class Indian Order of Merit and Jemadar Mohammad Arabi, the 2nd Class of the same order.

The Battalion remained at Paradis until 22 March when the Bareilly Brigade took over trenches from 24th Brigade, 8th Division and it came into Brigade Reserve at Cameron Lane.

Lieutenant F. A. de V. Robertson, I.A.R.O., and 17 men joined the Battalion on 21 March: and Major G. J. Davis, 22nd Punjabis, on 28 March: the latter was reposted to the 59th Rifles, F.F. on 3 April. About this time an issue of rubber trench boots was received and proved of great value in the wet trenches. The Indian pattern mule transport carts also were replaced by limbered waggons drawn by horses and a Maltese cart issued for Mess use: these were far more suitable.

On 30 March the Brigade was relieved in trenches by the Sirhind Brigade and marched to billets at Pacquat.

On 2 April the following reinforcement arrived: 54th Sikhs, F.F., one Indian officer and 62 other ranks 82nd Punjabis, one Indian officer and 31 other ranks, and on 6 April, Captain E. C. Creasy, Special Reserve, and Lieutenant C. M. Longbotham, 72nd Punjabis, reported their arrival for duty with the Battalion.

On 11 April the Bareilly Brigade relieved the Ferozepur Brigade in the line: Headquarters and two companies of the Battalion, with two companies of the Black Watch, attached, relieved the 129th Baluchis in Seaforth Road trenches. Two companies of the Battalion formed part of the Brigade Reserve. The Battalion remained in this portion of the line until 28 April when it was relieved by the 6th Battalion Gordon Highlanders and the 2nd Scots Guards. During this period a great deal of work was done in the construction of new trenches and in wiring, the weather being on the whole very fine and ground rapidly drying: existing trenches were greatly strengthened, communication and inspection trenches added, and dug-outs made. Much useful patrol work also was carried out. Both our own and the enemy artillery and trench guns were active most of the time and casualties were of daily occurrence.

On 15 April Major J. W. Milne, 82nd Punjabis, left the Battalion on being posted to the 41st Dogras. On 20 April Captain S. B. Pope left the Battalion to join the Meerut Divisional Signal Company.

On 25 April Captain J. Y. Tancred was seriously wounded while with a working party in Home Counties trench, and lost the sight of one eye. On 27 April Captain C. H. Elliot, who had only rejoined the Battalion on 20 April (he had been wounded in the shoulder on 9 December 1914) was killed in a most unlucky manner. He was superintending the firing of rifle grenades, and had fixed a grenade ready to fire it and was about to press the trigger, when a chance bullet from an enemy sniper struck the grenade and exploded it. Captain Elliot was killed instantly, and the man helping him was severely wounded.

On 29 April the Battalion moved to Leslobes, and on 30 April went to billets in La Couture.

The following additional awards for gallantry had been announced up to this date:

Indian Order of Merit 1st Class	One
Indian Order of Merit 2nd Class	One
Indian Distinguished Service Medals	Eight

On 4 May, H.R.H. The Prince of Wales paid the R.H. Battalion a surprise visit and spent about an hour with the officers and men. He was introduced and spoke to several Indian officers, including Subadars Sohel Singh, I.O.M., Raj Talab, I.D.S.M., Harchand Singh, I.O.M., Jemadars Mohammad Arabi, I.O.M., Golodu, et cetera. He appeared to be very interested and asked many questions.

On 8 May 1915, the Battalion moved to a position just in rear (west) of the Orchard on the Rue-de-Bois, marching at 10 p.m. via Croix Barbée and taking up a position in the gridiron (trenches) just in rear of the Black Watch. For some time preparations for an advance had been going on, and the attack was to commence on 9 May. On this day the Dehra Dun Brigade was to make an attack – the Bareilly Brigade being in Divisional Reserve.

The attack of the Dehra Dun Brigade failed: our artillery bombardment made no impression on the German trenches, and the enemy were apparently fully informed of and were waiting for the attack. A second assault carried out by the Dehra Dun Brigade was equally unsuccessful and the Bareilly Brigade was ordered up to support it.

Two companies of the Battalion were ordered to occupy the Crescent trench (see map III). The communication trench leading to it, marked D on the sketch, had been very badly knocked about by enemy shell fire: in parts it was almost destroyed and in many places not more than two feet deep: however it had to be used. Meantime the enemy was shelling heavily both the assembly trenches, and this communication trench. In moving up it No. III Company lost heavily.

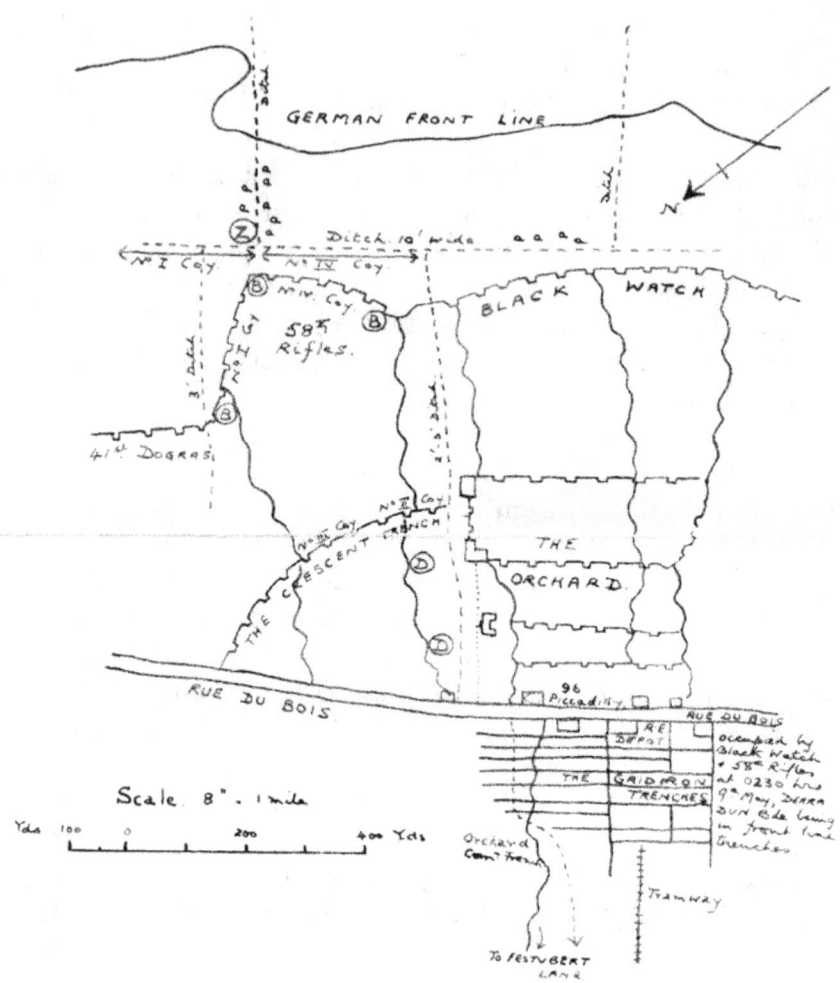

MAP. III. Action of 9th May. 1915. (RUE DU BOIS).

Lieutenant MacMillan was mortally wounded and 2 Indian officers, Subadar Bostan Khan and Jemadar Lal Khan, both 82nd Punjabis, were killed. At noon, orders were received that the Bareilly Brigade would carry out a fresh assault at 4 p.m. after a further bombardment by the artillery. The Battalion was ordered to occupy the trenches now held by the 4th Battalion Seaforth Highlanders, marked B-B on the sketch: the Black Watch being on the right and the 41st Dogras on the left. Accordingly Nos I and IV Companies occupied these trenches, Nos II and III being still in support in the Crescent. At 3.50 p.m., during the artillery bombardment, Nos I and IV Companies crossed the parapet and formed a line to right and left of the ditch marked 'Z'. Our artillery was firing very short and having no effect on the enemy, and these companies cane under heavy rile and machine gun fire. They pressed on, however, losing heavily as far as the ditch running parallel to our front, which was found to be full of water, in places 4½ feet deep, and some 10 feet broad. Here they were pinned to the ground both by the fire of the enemy and by our own artillery fire. So short were our guns firing that the enemy sat up on their parapet and shot down our men as they pressed on. Further advance was impossible and when the artillery ceased firing at 4 p.m. our men in the open had to take cover in water nearly up to their necks in any depressions in the ground they could find. Nos II and III Companies were now ordered up to fill the front line trenches and two companies of the 4th Royal Highlanders also came up: the front line was thus much too crowded in view of the fact that further advance was impossible. Our machine guns continued to fire on the enemy trenches in order to make the enemy keep their heads down: but one gun was completely knocked out by a shell and the whole team killed or wounded: the other gun continued in action in spite of heavy shelling. About 5 p.m. Nos I and IV Companies began to creep back to the trenches: some got in through holes dug under the parapet, others came over the top, but many were wounded in so doing. The attack of the Bareilly Brigade failed completely, as did that of the first Division on its right. When darkness fell the stretcher bearers, under Lieutenant S. Gordon, I.M.S., moved out and succeeded in bringing back all our wounded and many of the Seaforth Highlanders and Black Watch who were lying out in front of our trenches.

At 11.30 p.m. the Leicestershire Regiment relieved the Battalion that moved back to dug-outs in Forrester Lane.

Our casualties were very heavy. Three British officers were severely wounded: vizt: Major A. G. Thomson, Captain G. S. Bull, M.C., and Lieutenant A. MacMillan, who died the same night. Two Indian officers were killed and 5 wounded: 38 other ranks killed and 197 wounded.

In this attack of the Bareilly Brigade it was realised by all ranks, even to the Indian Corps Commander, that the task was impossible: but it had to be carried through in conjunction with the attacks of the Divisions on the right and left. In thanking the troops for their behaviour throughout this day the Indian Corps Commander well described the attack of the Bareilly Brigade as one of 'disciplined valour'.

The Battalion remained in trenches and dug-outs in the vicinity of Forrester's Lane and Croix Barbée from 10 to 16 May.

During this period the following reinforcements joined: Lieutenant F. B. Deane-Spread, I.A.R.O., 2nd Lieutenant J. Mackay, I.A.R.O., 11 other ranks of the 66th Punjabis, 49 other ranks of the 82nd Punjabis, 20 other ranks of the 58th Rifles, F.F.

On the night 15/16 May the attack on the German line was renewed. The Garhwal Brigade of the Meerut Division was in front: the Sirhind Brigade (attached temporarily to the Meerut Division) being in support and the Bareilly Brigade in reserve. This attack failed: but the 2nd Division of the 1st Corps on the right was partially successful. At 1 p.m. on 16th orders were received that the Bareilly Brigade would relieve the Garhwal Brigade in the front line, and at 8.30 p.m. the Battalion relieved the 2/3rd Gurkhas, in trenches south-west of the Orchard. The enemy shelled the line all night and the whole of the 17th. On 18 May the attack on our right was still progressing and the shelling of our trenches continued. On 20th the shelling was much less severe, and at night the 2/3rd Gurkhas relieved the Battalion which marched by companies to second line trenches at Croix Barbée. During this period our casualties were Jemadar Rakhmat and 5 other ranks killed: 4 Indian officers and 58 other ranks wounded; Captain F. F. Hodgson, 84thPunjabis (attached) was mortally wounded on 16 May, while in command of the Brigade machine guns in the Orchard trench and died the same night.

This period, from 9 to 19 May 1915 was probably the worst and most trying which the Battalion underwent during the whole war.

It was under almost incessant and most accurate gun fire, which our own artillery seemed powerless to neutralise. It was a constant struggle to keep the trenches sufficiently built up to afford protection and, in the constant expectation of counter-attack, the nerves of all ranks were at full stretch during the whole period. The casualties were very heavy and the visible results nil. By now most of the best of the original battalion and its reinforcements were gone: the reinforcements received at this time were chiefly men of other units containing a large percentage of old and unfit reservists, who were quite incapable of standing the strain of the strenuous warfare being carried on. Constant reports on useless reinforcements were sent in and many were returned to the Base almost as soon as they joined.

In this twelve days battle, during which we could only stand up and be hit, with little chance of retaliation, there was not much chance of individual brilliancy. The following, however, were specially brought to notice:

Lieutenant J. H. Milligan, who was constantly exposed carrying orders: and who directed the fire of the Battalion machine guns after their Indian officer had been wounded.

Captain E. S. C. A. C., Willis, D.S.O., and Captain G. S. Bull, led their companies with great gallantry in the attack on 9 May and extricated them skilfully when ordered to withdraw.

Jemadar Hawinda was conspicuous for fine leading of his platoon, and carried them forward with great gallantry until wounded.

No. 3405 Sepoy Lal Singh volunteered and successfully carried back an important message from Captain Willis under extremely heavy fire.

No. 3916 Sepoy Mehr Singh, and No. 2132 Sepoy Mota Singh, 82nd Punjabis both volunteered and carried several messages under heavy fire: both were wounded in doing so. No. 3136 Banta Singh, and No. 3187 Ram Saran, Headquarters orderlies, were constantly exposed to heavy fire carrying messages.

Nos 2747 Sepoy Wasawa Singh, 3131 Sepoy Phangan Singh, 3610 Sepoy Sucha Singh, and 3378 Lance-Naik Sudh Singh, fought their machine guns with great gallantry. On 9 May, one gun was smashed by a direct hit from a shell, and the other was under heavy fire throughout.

No. 2974 Lance-Naik Diwan Ali was especially prominent in directing the stretcher bearers, in rendering first aid and bringing in wounded. There were also numerous cases of wounded men of our own and other units being rescued and brought in under fire.

Jenadar Rakhmat (Yusufzi), who died on 17 May from wounds received in action, had shown most conspicuous courage throughout the war and a fine soldierly example.

Lieutenant J. H. Milligan, accompanied by Nos 3083 Naik Zarbaz (Yusufzi), 3804 Lance-Naik Misri Khan (P.M.), and 3515 Sepoy Gul Majan (Afridi), were also specially brought to notice for carrying out a close reconnaissance of the enemy's line under very adverse conditions with skill and daring.

The Battalion remained at Croix Barbée until the night 25/26 May when it marched to billets at La Couture.

The under mentioned officers had meanwhile joined the Battalion for duty: Lieutenant S. T. Gray, I.A.R.O., on 17 May; Captain C. B. Harcourt, 28th Punjabis, on 20 May; and Captain A. G. Lind rejoined the Battalion on 31 May.

Gas masks, vermorel sprayers and other precautions against gas attacks were issued at this time.

On 1 June, No. III Company marched three miles to La-Croix-Marmeuse to take part in an inspection of troops by the Prime Minister, Mr H. Asquith, who passed the line in a motor moving at twelve miles an hour: whereupon the company marched back three miles to billets.

On the night of 1/2 June the Battalion relieved the 1st Battalion 4th Royal Lancs in front line trenches by La Quinque Rue, and was in turn relieved on the night 6/7 June by the 41st Dogras and went into Brigade Reserve. It again relieved the 41st Dogras on the night 12/13 June, and remained in trenches until 18 June when it was relieved by the 6th Jats and marched to billets in Pacqaut. On the night 28/29 June the Battalion marched to trenches at Lansdowne Post, being in Brigade Reserve and on 9 July took over front line trenches in the Orchard from the 41st Dogras.

During this period orders had been received regarding strict investigation into any suspected cases of self inflicted wounds. This disgrace of malingering had been present from the commencement of the war and it may be safely said that few, if any, units were entirely free from it. It is a form of cowardice, which unless promptly and severely dealt with, spreads rapidly. The most common form of malingering was for a man to shoot himself through the palm of the hand or between the bones of the fore-arm or the foot. This is a thing that must be expected on long and arduous campaigns – and must be watched for and carefully guarded against.

On the night of the 11/12 July, No. 3457 Naik Safirallah (Yusufzai), accompanied by three men were sent on patrol to obtain information regarding the enemy's obstacles. They obtained the required information but while testing the enemy wire were seen and fired on, three of them being wounded. Naik Safirallah, although himself wounded, took the rifle of the most severely wounded man and covered his retirement: it was due to his skilful handling of his patrol, that they all got back with their arms and equipment. The Corps Commander recorded his appreciation of this piece of work in a message to the Brigade Commander. The bayonet strength of the Battalion was now 7 British and 10 Indian officers and 285 other ranks.

On 14 July, the Battalion was relieved by one company of the Royal Warwickshire Regiment (7th Division) and moved back to Les-Pures-Becques where most of the Indian battalions of the Corps were now in rest billets. Here it remained until 21 July when it marched to billets at La-Motte-Baudet. On 30 July it marched to La Flanque, a post south of Laventie and came into Brigade Reserve. This period was spent in general rest and clearing-up and light work, especially physical exercise and close order drill.

On the night 1/2 August the Battalion relieved companies of 5th Scottish Rifles in trenches in front of Mauquissart – a strong company (116 ranks) of the 41st Dogras being in support at Manquissart post.

On 5 August prolonged cheering was heard from the enemy trenches: German national flags were exposed over their parapets and boards held up on which were written 'Warschau fallen in our hands'. Our trench mortars and artillery very soon reminded them that the war was not yet finished. During this period there were several casualties, amongst whom Subadar Raj Talab, was wounded on 6 August

On 17 August a draft consisting of Lieutenant J. O. Nicolls, 2nd Lieutenant J. W. E., I.A.R.O. 3 Indian officers and 213 other ranks joined the Battalion: of these 2 Indian officers and 88 other ranks were of the 54th Sikhs F.F., the remainder being from our own Depot in India. This draft was of good physique, well trained, and far above the average of recent reinforcements from various sources.

The Battalion was relieved by the 39th Garhwalis on 17 August and went to billets in La-Belle-Croix, where it remained for one week and gave great assistance to the local farmers in harvesting the crops, for which the latter were duly grateful while the men, especially the Sikhs, thoroughly enjoyed the recreation and the temporary exchange of sword (bayonet) for the sickle.

The Battalion relieved the 2/3rd Gurkhas in trenches on 25 August and was in turn relieved by the 1st Battalion, 4th Seaforth Highlanders on 5 September and went into billets in Rugby Road. During this period, owing to information given by a German deserter of the 13th Bavarian Regiment, who gave himself up on 28 August, a strong enemy attack preceded by gas and exploding of mines said to be under our front line trenches was expected. It did not materialise, although much movement was observed and the enemy trenches were constantly full.

On 27 August a reinforcement of 2 British officers (Captain K. B. Mackenzie, and 2nd Lieutenant C. M. Durnford), 4 Indian officers and 162 other ranks of the 123rd (Outram's) Rifles joined the advance Depot and were brought into trenches on 1 September. On 5 September Captain J. H. Henderson, and Captain A. Flagg (Special Reserve) reported their arrival for duty. Captains A. G. Lind, and E. S. C. Willis, D.S.O., had left the Battalion during the previous month, the former sick and the latter as Instructor at the Cadet School at St Omar. Captain G. C. V. M. Wardell, who had been wounded on 10 March, also rejoined for duty with the Battalion.

The Battalion was at Rugby Road until 12 September when it relieved the 9th Gurkhas in front line trenches between Winchester Road and the moated Grange. During the periods out of trenches large working parties had been provided for the burying of telephone cables and work on trenches, everything pointing to an early resumption of hostilities. On 18 September the Battalion was relieved by the 1st Battalion Seaforth Highlanders and returned to the former billets in Rugby Road.

The Battalion was now not far short of full war strength but could only muster a bayonet strength of 582. The distribution at this time is shown below:

	British Officers	Indian Officers	Indian Other ranks
Trench Strength	10	15	562
At Advanced Depot	1	1	33
In Brigade Area	1	1	94
In Divisional Area			16
Elsewhere			17
Total	12	17	722

On 20 September the Bareilly Brigade was inspected by Field Marshal Lord Kitchener, K. G., who walked up and down the ranks of the Battalion. There were no speeches made.

On 22 September confidential orders were received for operations, which were to commence on 25th at dawn. These operations, known afterwards at the Battle of Loos, cost the Indian Corps in general, and the Bareilly Brigade in particular, exceedingly heavy losses.

On the evening of 24 September the Battalion which was in Brigade Reserve relieved the 9th Gurkhas in Ind 5 B sub-section –its strength being, British officers 9, Indian officers 12, other ranks 581. At about 3.50 a.m. on 25 September, the front line of the Bareilly Brigade, consisting (from left to right) of the Black Watch, the 1/4th Black Watch (Territorials) and the 69th Punjabis, advanced to the attack. The orders for the 58th Rifles were to occupy the front line held by the Black Watch immediately that Battalion went over the parapet. This was done: the line being occupied by about 6 a.m. The initial attack was most successful: in fact, so far did our first line advance that it was very shortly out of sight.

At 6.15 a.m., No. II Company (P.M.) under Lieutenant Nicolls on the left, and No. IV Company (P.M.s of the 123rd Rifles) under Captain Mackenzie, and 2nd Lieutenant C. M. Durnford on the right, crossed the parapet and advanced some 400 yards. No. II Company here went ahead, and No. IV Company, whose commander, Captain Mackenzie was now 'missing', stayed in the line marked 'A' on map IV, where they commenced to dig in. While advancing alone to reconnoitre a trench to his front Lieutenant Nicolls was killed by a bomb: this was at the end of the Winchester road, marked 'C' on the sketch. No. I Company (Pathans) under Captain Wardell and 2nd Lieutenant Deane-Spread and No. III Company (Sikhs and Dogras) under Captains Harcourt and Flagg, together with Battalion Headquarters, now came up and pushed through Nos II and IV Companies and working up the communication trench east of point 'C', reached the German second line, which they occupied on the line 'B-B' and began to consolidate. Here it became apparent that the attack of the Garhwal Brigade, on the right of the Bareilly Brigade, had failed to make sufficient ground for the Bareilly Brigade to advance further without unduly exposing its right flank. At about

10.30 a.m. parties of the 12th Rifle Brigade, whose role, it was understood, was to form a defensive flank on the left of the Bareilly Brigade, began to come upon the right of No. IV Company and an order was heard "12th Rifle Brigade close on your right." This Battalion appears to have closed on its right, exposing our left flank and very shortly afterwards the enemy heavily attacked this flank, and our line began to fall back. No. II Company, under Subadar Tikka Khan, made great efforts to hold up the enemy but expended all their bombs and all the enemy bombs (about 35) which they could find. The enemy's attack was well organised and vigorously pushed and by noon there was nothing left but to get back to the original line in as good order as possible. On muster being taken was found that 8 British and 6 Indian officers and 246 other ranks were killed, wounded or missing. The remainder of the Battalion under 2nd Lieutenant C. M. Durnford (the sole surviving British officer of those who had gone into action) was relieved in trenches at 6 a.m. on 26 September and marched back to billets at Pont du-Hem.

The above account of this disastrous action is necessarily incomplete and unconnected owing to the loss of all British and Indian officers who were in a position to give a connected account of what orders were given, and what actually took place. The whole of Battalion Headquarters were killed or missing and with them all orders and papers received and issued from the time the action started. There is no doubt that Lieutenant-Colonel

Davidson-Houston and his Adjutant, Lieutenant J. H. Milligan, lost their lives in a gallant and successful attempt to cover the withdrawal of the left of our line; in which the remainder of Battalion Headquarters, assisted by some of Nos I and III Companies led by Subadar Sohel Singh (bravest of the brave) and Jemadar Yar Dil, took part and were probably killed to a man.
The action of the officer commanding the Battalion in advancing to the support of the Black Watch, apparently without orders, has been questioned and criticised in the history of this action as

MAP IV. MAUQUISSART. (BATTLE OF LOOS) 25th SEPT. 1915.

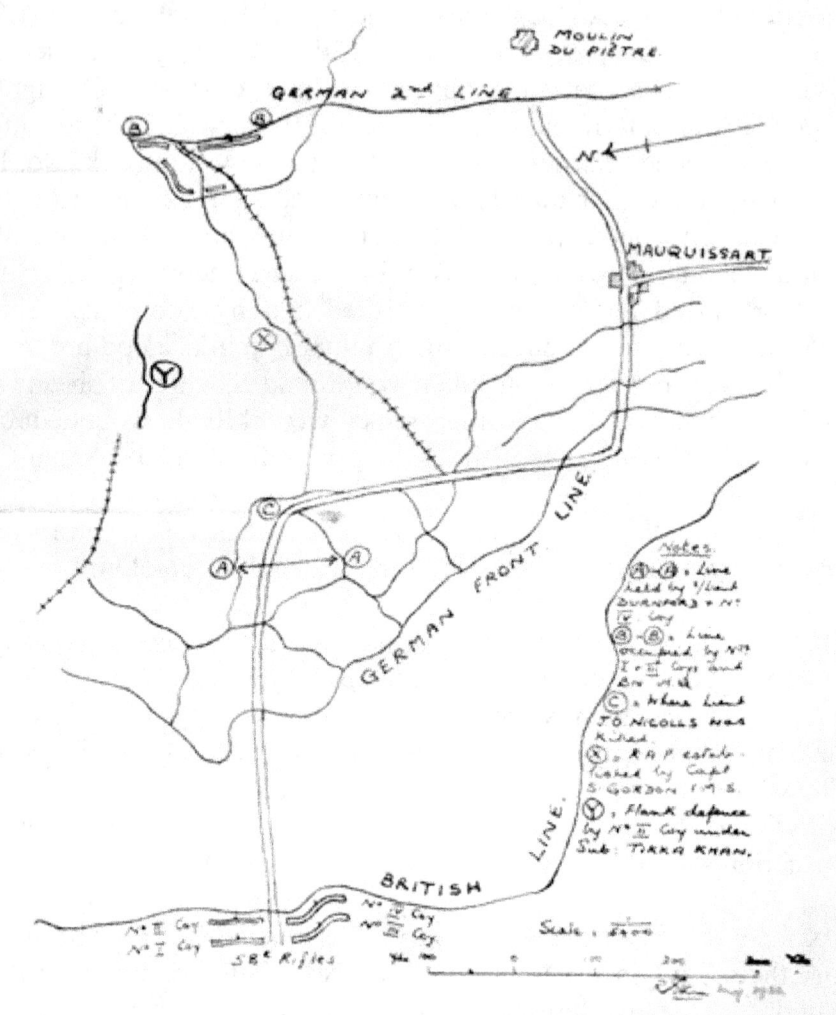

recorded in *The Indian Corps In France* by Lieutenant-Colonel J. W. E. Merewether and Sir J. E. Smith, Bart[2]: in the first edition of which work a very crude and inaccurate account is given of this particular episode. As the result of further enquiries and evidence, (which, however, should have been obtained prior to printing the first edition) the Second Edition contains a much fairer and more professional account of the movements of this Battalion (see preface to second edition, page xv and pages 448 to 453 of the book). In any case no one who knew Colonel Davidson-Houston, his splendid character and fine soldierly qualities, would doubt for one instant that he ordered his Battalion to advance without very good reason and without previously making every attempt to inform his Brigadier of his action.

As regards the action as a whole certain points appear obvious.
There was no organised method of 'mopping up' the captured trenches as the front line advanced such as became a *sine qua non* in all attack orders later on. The lines appear to have advanced as far as possible without clearing the trenches of the enemy, of whom a large number must have remained concealed in dug-outs whence they issued at odd times, especially during the enemy counter-attack and caused us considerable loss. Lieutenant Nicolls was certainly killed by enemy in a trench, which the first line has passed over: and Captain Mackenzie also, who with an orderly, had gone down a side trench to reconnoitre: and neither were ever seen again.

A unit of the Brigade on the left of the Bareilly Brigade was detailed to protect the exposed left flank of the Bareilly Brigade – which flank became more exposed the further the troops penetrated the German lines. This flank protection was not forthcoming. And in this the old Punjab Frontier Force adage, 'Never trust your flank to another unit,' is well exemplified.

---

[2] J. W. Bereseford Mereweither & Frederick E. Smith, Earl of Birkenhead, *The Indian Corps In France* (London, J Murray, 1919). The second edition was published in 1921. (JW ed.)

The officers commanding battalions of the Bareilly Brigade appear to have gone into action with the fixed idea that they were to make ground to the front as far as possible and exploit success: that reinforcements and an ample supply of bombs and appliances necessary for consolidating ground won, would be rapidly pushed up as soon as the initial success of the advance was assured. No reinforcements, nor material was sent in the four to five hours, which elapsed between the initial success and the withdrawal. It later transpired that the role to be played by the Indian Corps was that of a feint attack demonstration designed to draw off German Reserves from the real attack further south by Lens and Loos: but not one of the commanding officers of the Brigade appears to have been aware of this fact until after the action was over. Had they realised this, their action would probably have been more cautious and the general result would have been far more effective. The success attained was apparently unexpected and was not exploited by higher command. The only gratification the troops were able to extract from their fine initial successes was the mention, in the order of the day, that the Indian Corps had fulfilled its role in a very satisfactory way.

Of the part played by the Battalion in this action little more can be said. The morale vas very high and the advance carried out with great dash. Of individual deeds of gallantry no one can speak with certainty. The last stand of Lieutenant-Colonel Davidson-Houston and his small devoted band of officers and men is beyond all praise, and their memory will live in this Battalion as a noble example of self-sacrifice. Captain S. Gordon, I.M.S., again distinguished himself, advancing with the front line troops and establishing his aid post in a German aid post near the enemy second line, which he found full of useful appliances, and where he treated and evacuated numerous wounded with his accustomed skill. He later received tardy recognition by the award of the Military Cross, and No. 2934 Sepoy Mohammad Amin (P.M.) who directed the stretcher bearers with considerable daring, was awarded an I.D.S.M. Of the British and Indian officers not mentioned above Captain Flagg and 2nd Lieutenant Deane-Spread were killed: Captain Wardell was severely wounded: Captain Harcourt was captured, Jemadar Din Mohammad (123rd Rifles) was killed: Subadar Lal Singh and Subadar Karam Dad

(123rd Rifles) were wounded; Subadar Bhag Singh was severely wounded and captured. This Indian officer was well treated by the enemy: he was released early in 1918 being obviously unfit for any further service, sent to a convalescent home in Switzerland, and was repatriated in November 1918 after the Armistice. Thus for the second time in the war the Battalion lost its Commanding Officer and Adjutant in the same action. Through the death of Lieutenant-Colonel Davidson-Houston the Battalion experienced its greatest loss in the war. Practically all his service had been passed in the Battalion, to which he was devoted. Its welfare and success he had continually at heart and all ranks realised this and looked up to him with an affection and confidence, which was inspiring. He was probably as fine a leader of men as could be found: full of determination and resource: of encouragement and example in difficulties, of praise in success: never sparing himself, and with a sense of duty which was unsurpassed. A very gallant and distinguished officer, Major (now Major-General) A, G. Wauchope C.B., C.M.G., D.S.O. who commanded the Black Watch and who was closely connected with Lieutenant-Colonel Davidson-Houston in all actions in France in which their two battalions fought side by side, wrote of him:

> On many occasions I have been in action with Colonel Davidson-Houston: I have known no finer Commanding Officer. I have met no leader of greater resource. I have served with no soldier more brave, no man more straightforward, no officer of more just judgement. These qualities he showed in every battle.

These are true words, spoken from the heart: and we who served under him know how true they are.

From *the Times*, April 1916:

> Lieutenant-Colonel Charles Elrington Duncan Davidson-Houston, D.S.O., 58th Rifles, I.A., who was returned as 'Wounded and missing' on September 25 last, and is now unofficially reported 'Killed in action' on that date, was the youngest son of the late Rev. B. C. Davidson-Houston. MA, vicar of St John's Sandymount, Ireland, and chaplain

to the Lord Lieutenant. Born on January 21, 1878, he was educated in England and Germany. He entered the Indian Army in 1893, being promoted to Captain in 1902, Major in 1911, and temporary Lieutenant-Colonel in 1914. During this period he saw active service on the North-West Frontier of India –Tochi–1897-8 (medal and clasp), in Waziristan 1901-2 (clasp), on North-West Frontier, 1902 (slightly wounded). He was appointed Brigade Major of the Kohat Brigade in 1910, and of the Quetta Brigade in 1913, and acted as assistant secretary of the Durbar Committee at Delhi in 1911 (medal). He succeeded to the command of his regiment, the 58th Rifles, Frontier Force, L.A., after the death, in action, at Festubert, on October 31, 1914, of the then Commanding Officer, Lieutenant-Colonel W. E. Venour. Lieutenant-Colonel Davidson-Houston had commanded his regiment ever since with conspicuous ability, being in all the actions in which this regiment has taken part at Festubert in October and again in November, 1914; at Givenchy, December, 1914, where he gained the D.S.O., at Neuve Chapelle, at Richebourg l'Avoué, and finally at Manquissart on September 25 last, where, it is feared, he, together with several of his officers, fell fighting to the last in a gallant attempt to hold the German trenches which had been won that day, and from which the rest of the Brigade was forced to retire in the face of an overwhelming counter-attack. Lieutenant-Colonel Davidson-Houston married, in 1907, Constance Isabelle Burton, daughter of the late Professor Robert Caesar Childers.

Lieutenant J. H. Milligan was appointed Adjutant shortly after the death of Captain W. McM. Black in action 31 October 1914. He was an officer who had greatly endeared himself with all ranks by his cheery genial manners and fine example in work and games.

Mention in this history must also be made of Subadar Sohel Singh, I.O.M., whose death was a great loss to the Battalion.

Enlisted in 1901 his educational attainments caused him to be taken into the Battalion office, where, chiefly by his own abilities he became one of the best Adjutant's clerks that the Battalion has had.

All the time he was in the office he maintained and improved his professional knowledge and on promotion to Jemadar on 13 August 1914 proved himself a splendid leader. He was a true Sikh: loyal and devoted to those whose salt he had eaten, simple and straight-forward in thought, word and action, as brave as only a man can be who thinks of his duty and not of himself.

These three officers, whose gallantry and devotion are so inadequately recorded above, and whose memory will live forever in our hearts, are typical of those who have made our Battalion an entity of which to be proud: and their example something to admire and follow.

At dawn on 26 September the Dehra Dun Brigade relieved the Bareilly Brigade in the line – the Battalion strength 2 British and 2 Indian officers, 335 other ranks, including the advanced Depot, went into billets at Pont-du-Hem. The next day Captain S. B. Pope rejoined from duty with the General Staff Account Division and assumed temporary command. On 29th, the Battalion marched to La Gorgue and on 1 October to Gorre, where it came into Brigade Reserve. The following officers joined at Gorre: Captain A. G. Lind who assumed temporary command: Captain E. S. C. Willis, D.S.O.; 2nd Lieutenant A. J. O'Connor, I.A.R.O. On 6 October the Battalion relieved the 69th Punjabis in front line trenches, to the south of Givenchy Les-la-Bassée. On 9th the enemy exploded a series of mines under the trenches of the Black Watch on our left and made a small attack, which was repulsed. Our trenches were subjected to some shelling and a number of men wounded: 2nd Lieutenant A. J. O'Connor was slightly wounded and evacuated.

On 11 October the Battalion was relieved by the 39th Garhwal Rifles and marched to billets at Les Choquaux.

The following officers now joined the Battalion: Lieutenant-Colonel E. R. B. Murray, 90th Punjabis who assumed command on 13 October, Lieutenant G. C. Bampfield, 90th Punjabis on 12.10.15, Lieutenant A. Saunders, I.A.R.O., on 12.10.15, Captain H. J. Davson, 82nd Punjabis and Lieutenant Todd, 93rd Burmah Infantry on 13.10.15.

Captain S. B. Pope, left the Battalion on 13 October to resume his appointment with the General Staff Meerut Division.

The strength of the Battalion was now 10 British and 9 Indian officers, 575 other ranks – a number of men who had been evacuated sick or slightly wounded having rejoined, also others who had been reported missing on 25 September and who had become mixed up with other units, and one or two drafts who arrived from rest camps and salvage companies. Amongst these were included representatives of the 54th Sikhs F.F., the 123rd Rifles, the 66th, 76th and 82nd Punjabis. The Battalion was reorganised into companies and platoons, men of the various battalions being kept together as far as possible.

On 19 October the Battalion marched to Calonne and on 20th to Paradis where it remained in billets until 24th when it came into Brigade Reserve at Richelourg St Vaast. On 29 October it moved to Vielle Chapelle and on 2 November relieved the 33rd Punjabis in front line trenches in Ind 4 A sub-section. This was the last tour of trenches in France as the Indian Corps was now under orders to proceed to other theatres of the war.

On 6 November the Battalion handed over its line to the 8th Battalion Sherwood Foresters and marched to crossroads near Lestrem where motor buses were waiting: in these it was transported to Boeseghenn and thence marched to billets in Widdebrouck: strength 7 British 16 Indian officers 469 other ranks. On 11 November Lieutenant-General Sir C. Anderson, commanding the Indian Corps, and members of his staff, visited the Battalion and said goodbye to British and Indian officers. On 13 November the Battalion was moved to La Pierrére and on 18 November to Febrin Palpart.

The following officers had now joined the Battalion: Captain R. de W. Waller, 108th Infantry on 16.11.15, Major G. E. Hardie and Captain W. Odell both 123rd Rifles on 18.11.15.

The following officers left the Battalion: Captain E. S. C. Willis, D.S.O., on 22.11.13 to rejoin his appointment as Instructor at the Cadet School at General headquarters; Lieutenant Todd 93rd Burma Infantry to rejoin his battalion on 22.11.15; 2nd Lieutenant Roy-Smith, interpreter, to take up an appointment in the Army Service Corps. This officer joined the Battalion at Marseilles on 13 October 1914 and remained with it the whole time it was in France. He had become very popular with all ranks, for whose welfare and comfort he had worked unceasingly, getting billets and supplies. His duties as interpreter should not have taken him beyond the advance Depot of the Battalion, but he often voluntarily ran great risks in bringing rations to the trenches when work was heavy and officers few, he acquired an excellent working knowledge of Hindustani and frequently officiated at Quarter Master and in command of the advance Battalion Depot. On leaving the he took with him the gratitude and good wishes of all who had known him.

On 25 November H.R.H. The Prince of Wales held a parade of representatives of all Indian units and read them a gracious message from His Majesty the King (Appendix E). Five British and 5 Indian offers, 8 non-commissioned officers and 8 sepoys of the Battalion were present on this parade.

On 29 November the long delayed orders for entrainment were received and on 30th the Battalion marched to Lillers and entrained. It arrived at Marseilles at 2.30 a.m. on 3 December: strength 10 British 16 Indian officers, 552 other ranks. Here 5 Indian officers and 247 other ranks joined the battalion from the base Depot.

On 6 December the Battalion embarked on the SS *Ivernia*, on which also were the 33rd Punjabis, two companies Sappers and Miners and the Headquarters of Meerut Division, the Dehra Dun and Bareilly Brigades.

The journey to Port Said, where the Battalion disembarked on 14 December, was without incident. On the same day the Battalion entrained and arrived at Suez Camp, where it remained until 27 December, when it was moved to El Shatt on the east bank of the Suez Canal, where it remained until 23 January 1916.

CHAPTER III
Egypt and Sinai, 1916

On 8 January 1916 the Company of the 123rd Outram's Rifles, attached to the Battalion, left for Mesopotamia to reinforce the 104th Rifles. Its strength was 3 British officers (Major Hardie, Captain Odell and Lieutenant Durnford) 3 Indian officers and 184 other ranks. This Company had done excellent work with the Battalion and had formed a great friendship with men of the 58th Rifles F.F. which was later on to be cemented when the two battalions formed part of the same Brigade in Palestine.

On 25 January all ranks of the 54th Sikhs F.F. and the 82nd Punjabis, total 6 Indian officers and 231 other ranks, left the Battalion to join the 53rd Sikhs F.F. and the 82nd Punjabis respectively, en route to Mesopotamia. The reinforcements from these battalions had done splendid work, taken their full share in all the hardships, victories and losses while with the Battalion and will always be remembered with gratitude and respect.

Meantime the following joined the Battalion: 2nd Lieutenant A. I. G. McConkey on 5.1.16; 2nd Lieutenant G. G. Hills, I.A.R.O., on 18.1.16; 54 rank and file from the Depot in India on 1.1.16; 2 Indian officers and 120 rank and file from Marseilles on 8.1.16; 1 Indian officer and 15 other ranks from hospitals in England on 15.1.16.

The various units of the Indian Army Corps in France, which had been known as Force A, were now being distributed to various theatres of war. The Headquarter staffs of the Lahore and Meerut Divisions, together with their Brigade staffs had gone on to

Mesopotamia and some of the original units with them: there they were made up to strength by fresh units from India. But of the majority of the former units, some remained in Egypt, some went to East Africa, others returned to India or to Aden. The cavalry had all remained in France. The 58th Rifles F.F. was ordered to remain in Egypt and was temporarily attached to 31st Indian infantry Brigade. The east bank and the desert country to the east of the Suez Canal was now being put into a state of defence, it being Lord Kitchener's policy to defend Egypt proper and the Suez Canal from the eastern bank instead of using the Canal as an obstacle as had been done up to that time.

On 15 January 1916 two companies were moved to Gebel Murr, a low commanding hill, some seven miles east of Suez, which was being fortified. On 23 January the remainder of the Battalion marched to Gebel Murr in relief of the 2nd Bn, 8th Gurkhas. On 8 February it was in turn relieved by Patiala Imperial Service Infantry and marched to El Shatt, and on 11 February relieved the 2nd Bn, 2nd Gurkhas at Ayun Musa, some five miles south-east of Suez on the east bank of the Canal. Ayun Musa (the wells of Moses) consisted of a low sandy ridge some 2,000 yards long running from north to south and curling towards the west at its southern end. It was also being fortified. At its northern end were three groves of fine palm trees in which were several wells of brackish water; the peculiarity of this location was that the water issued from the tops of low hillocks on the ridge –the lower ground being quite dry. The Battalion was now definitely posted to the 20th Indian Infantry Brigade. It was engaged now and for several succeeding months in the construction of field works and defences in the southern sector of the Suez Canal defences. As much training and musketry as possible was also done. On 1 March the Battalion returned to El Shatt and took over duties from Patiala Imperial Service Infantry.

Captain H. J. Davson 82nd Punjabis left the Battalion on 7 March to join his own battalion in Mesopotamia.

On 6 March a reinforcement consisting of 1 Indian officer and 138 other ranks of the 55th Rifles F.F. and 20 other ranks from the Battalion Depot in India joined for duty. On 2 March the Battalion was relieved by the 23rd Sikh Pioneers and marched to the Quarantine station at the extreme southern end of the Canal, and two miles from Ayun Musa.

The strength of the Battalion at this time was 9 British and 11 Indian officers and 585 other ranks.

On 26 March an unpleasant incident occurred. Just before dusk a havildar of the 2nd Bn, 3rd Gurkhas, a detachment of which battalion was camped just outside the defences, went amok on account of some fancied grievance – shot two of his Gurkha officers and another havildar of his battalion, and then got into one of the trenches and began to shoot indiscriminately in all directions. This Sikh Company, thinking there was some alarm, on account of the sudden firing, turned out to take up alarm posts in their trenches and were promptly fired on by this Gurkha havildar from the rear and seven of them were wounded before they grasped the situation. Three other men of the Battalion, who also passed in the open, not understanding what was happening, were wounded. It was a very unpleasant situation as it was growing dark – the madman was somewhere under cover in a trench and his exact position could not be located. However, some men of the P.M. Company were brought up under cover of the trench parapet and at a given signal jumped over the top of the parapet and one of them bayoneted the madman just as he jumped up to fire. It was afterwards discovered in post-mortem examination that the havildar bad been wounded slightly in the head in France, and that a small portion of his skull had been for some time pressing on his brain, which was diseased, he was not responsible for his action.

On 27 March H.R.H. The Prince of Wales, who was making a tour of the Egyptian front, accompanied by General Sir W. R. Birdwood landed at the Ayun Musa, Quarantine Post, and stayed for half an hour talking with British and Indian officers.

On 1 April a reinforcement of 1 Indian officer and 157 other ranks under command of Lieutenant G. R. Dowland arrived from the Depot in India. The following officers also arrived for duty: Captain S. B. Pope, on 31.3.16 from France. Captain D. H. Acworth, M.C., 55th Rifles F.F. on 8.4.16.

On 12 April the Battalion handed over duties at Quarantine to the Alwar Imperial Service Battalion and on13 April marched to the plateau position, then in course of construction, and took over duties from the Gwalior Imperial Service Battalion: the strength of the Battalion being 12 British, 19 Indian officers and 735 other ranks.

The Battalion here heard with deep regret of the death on 28 March of Captain G. S. Bull, M.C., who, having partially recovered from the severe wound he received in France on 9 May 1915, had been appointed Adjutant of the rest camp at Sidi Bisher near Alexandria. He had greatly distinguished himself in all the fighting in which the Battalion had been engaged from the date it arrived in France until he was wounded. He was a born leader of men, gallant and full of determination, and his men would follow him anywhere. His death was largely the result of his wound.

On 20 April it was reported that the 2nd Battalion 3rd Gurkhas, who were engaged in building a fortified post in the vicinity of the wells at Bir Mabeuik, about fifteen miles east of the Canal, had come into contact with Turkish troops: in the evening about 5.30 p.m. a further report stated that a patrol of the battalion together with some Yeomanry, bad been fired on from close quarters and had suffered some casualties. Orders were received for 300 rifles of the 58th to move out at once in support. At 6.15 p.m. this column started under command of Major Lind, and arrived at Bir Mabeuik at 9.45 p.m. The distance of the march was twelve miles, over heavy sand. In the course of the night Lieutenant-Colonel Murray arrived at Bir Mabeuik with some Yeomanry and took over command. Two passes through the hills, dividing the interior of Sinai from the Suez Canal sandy plain, debouched into this plain some five miles east of Bir Mabeuik: the chief one being the Raha Pass. A reconnaissance of this Pass and the hills to its south was decided on. At 1 a.m. on 21st troops left in three columns covering five miles of front and penetrated the hills for some three miles, no enemy was encountered but a few shots were fired from long range. The troops withdrew in the afternoon arriving at Bir Mabeuik at 6.30 p.m. The day had been excessively hot and very little water was found. The column under Major Lind returned to the plateau next day arriving at 11 a.m. This was the first experience of desert work and had been very fatiguing: thirty-three miles of country had been covered in very hot weather in thirty hours, including hill picquetting, but only two men fell out. On 23 April a column of 300 rifles under Major Lind was again sent to Bir Mabeuik, and on the night 23/24 April moved out to the Raha Pass and picquetted the entrance to it before dawn. During 24th the column penetrated the Pass for some six miles. A few enemy were encountered and one picquet had a slight engagement on the right flank, but the enemy would not come to close quarters. The day was extremely hot, but fortunately water was found. The night was spent in bivouac, and on 25th the column withdrew, without being molested, to Bir Mabeuik: returning to the plateau on 26th.

On 27 April a draft of 50 men arrived from the Depot, in India, accompanied by Subadar Karam Singh, I.O.M., and Subadar Indar Singh, M.C., I.D.S.M. On 14 May a detachment of 320 rifles under Major Lind marched to Bir Mabeuik and took over that position from the Gwalior Imperial Service Battalion. On 15 May, Headquarters and the remainder of the Battalion relieved the Alwar Imperial Service troops at Ayun Musa, and on 25 May moved to El Shatt. On 29 May the detachment at Bir Mabeuik was relieved by the Patiala Imperial Service Infantry and joined Battalion Headquarters at El Shatt.

On 27 May Captain S. B. Pope left the Battalion to take up an appointment as G.S.O.III in the 2nd Australian and New Zealand Corps (ANZAC) in France. Captain Pope never joined the Battalion again but continued to hold staff appointments, for which he was admirably suited, with the ANZAC in France and with the 60th (London) Division in Palestine, until the Armistice. He was appointed G.S.O.I of the 60th Division and gained several honours and mentions. Thereafter he served on staff of the Quetta Division until 1923. His name was finally removed from the rolls of the 58th Rifles F.F. on his appointment as second in command 96th Infantry. Captain D. H. Acworth, M.C., 35th Rifles F.F., attached, also left to take up an appointment, as Staff Captain, Suez Base. On 31 May Lieutenant-Colonel E. R. B. Murray proceeded on leave to England and Major A. G. Lind took over temporary command of the Battalion.

On 3 June Lieutenant D. B. Mackenzie (I.A. on probation) arrived from the Depot in India with a draft of 50 men.

On 21 June Captain G. Bampfield handed over the adjutancy to Lieutenant Mackenzie and left the Battalion to rejoin his own battalion, 90th Punjabis, in Mesopotamia.

On 25 June the Battalion marched to Ayun Musa in relief of the 57th Rifles F.F. who had been ordered to East Africa. The Battalions met on the road and fraternised for half an hour before proceeding their separate ways. This move involved the transfer of the Battalion from the 20th Brigade to the 29th Brigade, under Brigadier-General P. C. Palin, C.M.G., D.S.O. The Battalion was still engaged in building and rebuilding defences: the idea seemed to be to get the Canal defences completed before any systematic training for troops was carried out. This simply meant that no real training was ever done because the defences could never be said to be complete – as soon as one was finished another had to be cleared of sand that had drifted in, or built up again where the sand had given way. It resembled the labours of Hercules, and was about as heartbreaking. However, a certain amount of musketry training was carried out, and occasionally sports were held.

On 20 July El Shatt and Port Tewfiq were bombed by enemy aeroplanes and a good many casualties occurred amongst camels, of which there was a large camp near El Shatt. Thereafter, for a month, enemy planes were active over the south end of the Canal.

About eighteen miles south-east of Ayun Musa was the Garad Pass through the hills to Nekhal, the capital of Sinai, which was held by the Turks. On the way to this pass and fifteen miles distant from the Ayun Musa were the wells of Bir-Abu-Tif, and this water, as well as the entrance to the Pass, was frequently reconnoitred by the County of London Yeomanry, as it was one of the few places whence an enemy might carry out an attack on Ayun Musa. About this time the Yeomanry had suffered casualties through scouts being ambushed by Bedouin snipers on several occasions. On 9 August two companies under Major Waller moved out to Bir-Abu-Tif by night, and concealed themselves there all through the 10th. In the evening the Yeomanry reconnaissance party arrived and bivouacked openly, as they had done before, with a view to reconnoitring the Garad Pass in the early morning of 11th, the infantry took up positions on the west side of the pass where the Yeomanry had encountered the enemy before. At dawn the Yeomanry appeared in the valley below and were fired on at long range by some 40 to 50 enemy, who, unfortunately, had occupied the hill on the east side of the pass. No casualties occurred and though unsuccessful it was very good training for the infantry.

On 23 August 1916 the Sikh Company under Major R. de W. Waller with Lieutenant G. R. Dowland was despatched to Somaliland. On the same day Lieutenant-Colonel E. R. B. Murray, who had been temporarily commanding the 20th Brigade since his return from leave, rejoined the Battalion and assumed command.

On 27 August the Battalion, less 300 rifles under Major Lind, moved to the Quarantine defence post on relief by the Patiala Imperial Service Infantry. The detachment under Major Lind marched to Bir Mabeuik and took over that post from the Alwar Imperial Service Infantry.

On 31 August the distribution of the Battalion overseas was:

	British Officers	Indian Officers	Indian Other Ranks
At Quarantine (Ayun Musa)	3	5	250
Bir Mabeuik	3	5	306
Somaliland (en route)	2	5*	188
Total	8	15*	744

*includes one sub-assistant surgeon

On 20 September it was announced that furlough to India for one month had been sanctioned for ten percent of the strength. A request for furlo for the Indian ranks had been put up by the Commanding Officer during the previous June. The war dragged on, but there was little of war in Egypt for those engaged on the defence of the Suez Canal: and no chance of distinction or getting away from the daily routine through the chances of war such as wounds. The men were becoming stale and home-sick; it was known that leave home was being given to British and Colonial troops. So the announcement of this furlough, short though it was for men who had to travel long distances to their home, often four or five days on foot after leaving the railway, was very welcome and gave the men something to look forward to and talk over.

On 3 October Battalion Headquarters at the Quarantine defence post were relieved by the 23rd Sikh Pioneers and marched to El Shatt rail-head where they relieved the Gwalior Imperial Service Infantry. On the same day the detachment at Bir Mabeuik was relieved by a detachment of the 23rd Pioneers and marched to El Shatt rail-head.

On 29 October a draft of 50 men under Captain R. B. Kitson arrived from the Depot in India. Captain Kitson had been appointed to the Burma Military Police just before the outbreak of War in 1914 and, greatly to his disappointment, had not been allowed to accompany the Battalion on service, but had been obliged to serve for two years in Burma. He had taken the first opportunity to rejoin his battalion.

On 1 December 1916, Captain S. Gordon, M.C., I.M.S., left the Battalion, having been appointed to the 123rd Indian Field Ambulance. Captain Gordon was posted to the Battalion at Chaman, in April 1914. He accompanied it to France and was with it in all its various actions and vicissitudes, and indefatigable in the discharge of his duties. His pluck and daring was a byword with all ranks: his hospital personnel would follow him anywhere. He was instrumental in saving many valuable lives, he earned mention many times for his personal bravery, and was awarded the Military Cross after the action on 25 September 1915. Nor was he less zealous in the care of the sick and the general health and hygiene of the Battalion. His departure was greatly regretted by all ranks, who regarded him with real affection.

On 1 December Captain M. J. Holgate, I.M.S., took over medical charge of the Battalion.

On 15 December 2nd Lieutenant J. Mackay, I.A.R.O., and 2nd Lieutenant G. P. Farley, I.A.R.O., with a draft of 37 men arrived from the Depot in India.

On 4 December Captain A. Saunders, I.A.R.O., left the Battalion to take up an appointment as Staff Captain Suez Base.

The Battalion was now ordered to move in relief of the 2nd Battalion, 3rd Gurkhas, to the two ports, Abu Zanima and Tor, situated on the east coast of the Gulf of Suez and respectively 60 and 120 miles south of Suez. Two companies were detailed for Abu Zanima, the other two companies with Battalion Headquarters going to Tor.

On 18 December the Battalion left El Shatt rail-head, and embarked at Port Tewfiq on the transport SS *Georgian*, which sailed the same evening, and arrived off Abu Zanima at dawn on 19 December. The steamer was too large to go alongside the half-finished pier, and, as there were no lighters or other means of landing men and animals, nothing could be done until the arrival of the Sinai Mining Company's tender, the *Argyll*. This small steamer arrived at dusk and early on 20 December the detachment, consisting of 3 British and 4 Indian officers and 306 other ranks under command of Major Lind, was disembarked and took over the post.

The SS *Georgian* sailed on 21 December and on 22 December Battalion Headquarters and two companies landed at Tor and took over from the 2nd Battalion 3rd Gurkha Rifles.

Abu Zanima is a small Arab settlement, with some pretensions to a harbour, where the headquarters of the Sinai Mining Company is located. Umbogma manganese mines, which are valuable, are situated in the hills some nineteen miles from Abu Zanima with which they are connected by a light railway for thirteen miles, and an aerial railway for six miles. When the war broke out the Mining Company was in course of constructing its headquarters, an aerial railway and a pier. When the Turks joined in the war they raided and partially burnt Abu Zanima, damaged the aerial railway to some extent, and retired some twenty miles into the hills, where they established picquets. Abu Zanima was reoccupied early in 1916 without opposition, and it was decided, in the interests of the Mining Company to place. a military garrison there so that work on the buildings and aerial railway might he carried on. The Battalion kept this detachment until the end of August 1917; its strength being reduced to one company as will be described later on. Frequent reconnaissances were made into the hills and up to the mines, but no serious opposition was ever encountered. The detachment rendered great assistance to the Mining Company in supplying voluntary paid labour in the reconstruction of buildings and roads and in re-claiming the steel cables and many portions of the aerial railway, which had become buried in debris brought down the nullahs during the past two rainy seasons. A good deal of musketry and useful training was also carried out.

Tor is a well-known international disinfection station at the southern end of the Gulf of Suez. It is here that all infectious cases of sickness, entering Egyptian waters, are landed and treated: also immigrants are landed and segregated – as are the majority of pilgrims from Mecca-Medina. It was occupied by the Turks who did no damage. Later on it was reoccupied by the British, and the Turks retired, offering little opposition. The Battalion held this detachment, which was later on reduced to one company, until early in September 1917. Nothing of any interest, occurred at Tor except the despatch of an escort under Captain R. B. Kitson at the end of March 1917 with a small military mission which visited the Monastery of Sainte Katherina on Mount Sinai: the oldest Monastery in the world – which had sheltered the Prophet Mohommad in his flight from Mecca, and had, for that reason, been immune from attacks by Mohommadans ever since. The mission was under orders of Colonel Lord Stradbroke, C.R.A., the southern Canal section, and its object was of a political nature. The mission and escort remained for four days at Mount Sinai, and having successfully accomplished its object returned to Tor.

About the time the Battalion took over the posts at Abu Zanima and Tor, our troops, advancing along the north coast of Sinai, were meeting with considerable success: the Turks were defeated at Magdaba and El Arish and had retired on Gaza and Beersheba.

Our agents in the Sinai Peninsula reported the Turkish detachments were very dispirited and the local Bedouins inclined to be friendly. This indeed, was a necessity for the latter as the Turks had hitherto supplied them with grain, and if they were unable to obtain food stuffs from the Turks they must either starve or submit to the British in order to supplement their very meagre local supplies by coastal trade with Egypt. During January 1917 most of the Turkish detachments were withdrawn from the Sinai Peninsula, and the majority of the Bedouin tribes in that district made their submission and took an oath of allegiance to the Sultan of Egypt: and trade was renewed. The restoration of the valuable charcoal trade between Abu Zanima and Suez was much appreciated at Suez.

The detachments at Abu Zanima and Tor were relieved on 1 September 1917 by infantry of the Egyptian Army, and rejoined Battalion Headquarters as will be narrated later on.

On 4 February 1917, Lieutenant-Colonel E. R. B. Murray left the Battalion to take over command of the 29th Indian Infantry Brigade. He published the following Battalion Order:

> On leaving the Regiment which I have had the honour to command for fifteen months on active service in France and Egypt, I wish to thank all the British and Indian officers and the non-commissioned officers for the loyal help they have always given me: and also all ranks for their loyal devotion to duty, which has well maintained the good name and honour of the 58th Rifles, F.F., and the fine traditions of the Frontier Force. I wish especially to include the Sikh Company under Captain R. de. W. Waller in Somaliland. I wish also to express my thanks to Temporary Major J. D. M. Flood and all ranks at the Depot, Ferozepore, who have worked so hard to keep the well-being and efficiency of the Regiment in the Field.

While much regretting his departure, all ranks were gratified at the promotion of Lieutenant-Colonel Murray to command of the Brigade in which the Battalion was serving.

CHAPTER IV
Palestine, 1917

The command of the Battalion was taken over by Major A. G. Lind with effect from 5 February 1917.

On the same date orders were received to reduce the strength of the garrison at Tor and Abu Zanima to one company each, and for Headquarters and the remainder of the Battalion, with the machine guns, to embark for Suez. Accordingly on 7 February, Battalion Headquarters, 1 British and 3 Indian officers and 117 other ranks, and two machine guns, were embarked on the SS *Trewellard* and sailed the same evening for Abu Zanima. On 8 February, 1 British and 1 Indian officer and 93 other ranks were embarked from Abu Zanima. There was the usual difficulty at Abu Zanima of embarking troops and animals. The steamer was unable to approach nearer than three-quarters of a mile to the shore and no arrangements had been made for lighters or rafts. The troops and animals were brought out to the steamer in Arab dhows, the mules having to be slung off the half-finished pier, a most perilous performance both for animals and men.

On 9 February the troops disembarked, and the same day crossed to the east bank of the Canal and were railed to the Quarantine station, where they went into camp.

While waiting at El Shatt the Commanding Officer was informed by Brigadier-General A. Pitt, commanding, the 6th Mounted Brigade, that the wing of the Battalion would join a mobile column, which was shortly to march to Nekhl, the chief town in the interior of Sinai, some seventy-five miles distant. The wing of the Battalion would remain under the 29th Indian Infantry

Brigade for administration, and under the 6th Mounted Brigade for tactical purposes.

On the evening of 9 February, Lieutenant D. B. Mackenzie, and Lieutenant R. G. Ekin, (55th Rifles, F.F.) marched in from Bir Mabeuik with a company of the 55th Rifles F.F. which had arrived in Egypt about one month previously as a reinforcement and in place of the Sikh Company in Somaliland. It was a composite company consisting of Khattacks, Yusufzai and Punjabi Mohommadans, with 4 Indian officers. Its strength was 218 rifles and it formed a most useful addition.

On 13 February A Company (Sikhs and Dogras) under Lieutenant D. B. Mackenzie moved out to Bir-Abu-Tif (seventeen miles) with orders to move on next day and picquet the hills on either side of the Garad Pass for the passage of the convoy on 15th and of the mounted column on 16 February. On 14 February the convoy of 700 camels marched to Bir-Abu-Tif, escorted by one company of the Battalion, 50 rifles of the 101st Grenadiers under Captain H. C. Laird and 33 rifles of the Imperial Camel Corps (British) under Captain Lord Winterton. Battalion Headquarters accompanied, the whole convoy and escort being under orders of Major A. G. Lind. On 15 February the convoy and escort reached Henaik (sixteen miles) without incident. On 16 February the convoy and escort advanced to Ain-Sudr (eleven miles). A few enemy camelry sniped the advance guard but did not wait to be driven off. The whole route, from the entrance to the Garad Pass to where the track debouched on to open uplands at Ain-Sudr, was a mass of hills which had to be picquetted; the picquets having to remain in position until the mounted column, which had advanced from Bir Abu-Tif on this date, had passed through them. On arrival at Ain-Sudr, which had been a Turkish entrenched camping ground, the officer commanding escort had only one platoon in hand; fortunately the camp was discovered to be empty. The mounted column did not arrive until an hour after sunset, and the first picquets, which had been in position for some ten hours, had considerable difficulty in finding their way to the camp in dark and rain.

On 17 February the mounted column moved to Natila (nineteen miles) with the convoy which was escorted by Lord Winterton's Camelry and 50 rifles under Lieutenant Ekin. The remainder of the escort remained at Ain-Sudr. On 19 February the column returned from Nekhl. Another mounted column of Australian Light Horse, which was supposed to be cooperating from the north with General Pitt's column, had arrived at Nekhl on the night of 18th, found it practically empty, and secured any loot which was to be had!

On 20 February the column returned to Ayun Musa. The convoy and escort arrived without incident on 22 February at Quarantine. Although practically no enemy had been met, the operation had been excellent training for the troops. Experience had been gained and the picquetting was remarkably good.

On 26 February a detachment consisting of 2 British officers, 5 Indian officers, 307 other ranks with two machine guns, under Lieutenant McConkey, took over the post at Bir Mabeuik from the 101st Grenadiers. The Battalion was now split into five detachments. One company each at Las Khorai (Somaliland), Tor and Abu Zanima, practically two companies at Bir Mabeuik, Battalion Headquarters and remaining troops at Quarantine. It was an unsatisfactory position, and office work was tripled, but presumably it was a matter of expediency.

On 8 April a draft of 72 men under Havildar Baidullah Khan arrived from the Depot in India. On 9 April the detachment at Bir Mabeuik was relieved by Patiala Imperial Service Infantry. One company under Lieutenants Jameison and Farley was sent to Ayun Musa: half a company under Lieutenant Ekin went to Gebel Murr with orders to dismantle that post and salve all valuable property.

The other half company rejoined Battalion Headquarters, which on the same date, had moved to El Shatt. On 26 April the half company under Lieutenant Ekin, having completed its work at Gebel Murr, rejoined Battalion Headquarters.

On 27 April, Lieutenant R. F. Jameison reported his departure to join the Royal Flying Corps.

On 24 April, fourteen cases of Bubonic plague were reported in the Gurkhas' camp at El Kubri and on 29 April some dead rats were found near El Shatt Camp, which were supposed to be plague infected. On 1 May Battalion Headquarters and troops in camp at El Shatt were ordered to shift camp one mile to the east of the post, and no one was allowed to leave camp in the direction of the Canal except on duty. The Battalion remained in segregation camp from now until relieved on 23 June, a considerable amount of training was carried out and specialists trained in machine gun, bombing and signalling. The Battalion was not affected by the plague.

Towards the end of May furlough to India was sanctioned. Dogras and Afridis were allowed two months, and other classes two months leave from the date of arrival in India. The first batch of furlough men, 100 of all ranks and followers left for India on 13 June.

A draft of 40 men from the Depot in India arrived on 31 May.

On 8 May the Sikh Company returned from Somaliland and went into camp at Suez, rejoining Headquarters in camp at El Shatt on 16 June.

On 22 June orders were received to relieve the two companies at Tor and Abu Zanima by sending the other two companies with Battalion Headquarters to replace them: and Battalion Headquarters to move to Ismailia.

The Battalion, which since the return of the Sikh Company, now consisted of five companies, was reorganised as follows:

A Company – Captain R. B. Kitson,
2 platoons Dogras and 2 platoons Yusufzais.

B Company – Lieutenant, acting Captain, G. R. Dowland,
4 platoons Punjabi Mohommadans.

C Company – Major R. de W. Waller,
4 platoons Sikhs.

D Company – Lieutenant R. G. Ekin,
1 platoon P.M.s of 55th Riles F.F.
1 platoon Afridis
1 platoon Yusufzais, 55th Rifles F.F.
1 platoon Khattaks, 55th Rifles F.F.

On 25 June the post at El Shatt was handed over on relief to the 101st Grenadiers and the Battalion, less detachments at Tor and Abu Zanima, crossed to Suez. On 26 June Battalion Headquarters moved by rail to Ismailia and camped on a sandy desert near the railway station, as the regular camping ground was occupied by the 2nd Battalion 3rd Gurkhas and 123rd (Outram's) Rifles, who formed part of the newly raised 234th Brigade, 75th Division. These battalions entrained for El Arish on 29/30 June and Battalion Headquarters moved to the camp lately occupied by the 123rd Rifles, a pleasant change. On 2 July, C and D Companies, which had remained at Suez, sailed for Abu Zanima and Tor respectively and on 5 July A and B Companies arrived thence at Ismailia. On 27 July, while at Ismailia, nine of the twenty-three Afridis, who deserted from their picquet in France on the night 2/3 March 1915, were handed over to Battalion charge, having been arrested in Persia and sent from India to undergo trial by Court-Martial. It was, however, impossible to get evidence to prosecute effectively, as most of those Afridis who could give evidence as to desertion, and all evidence as to apprehension of the prisoners were in India. Under these circumstances orders were received to return the prisoners to India, and they left on 3 August. The question of retaining Afridis in the Battalion had been exercising the mind of the Commanding Officer since February. The recruiting of Afridis ceased in 1915, owing to their unreliability. The old double company of Afridis was reduced to some 75 men including all those who had come from the 55th Rifles F.F. as a reinforcement, and there was an unduly large percentage of officers and non-commissioned officers amongst them.

They were unpopular with other classes owing to the disgrace they had brought on the name of the Battalion by the desertion of twenty-three of their number in France, and a subsequent attempt at desertion by some others early in 1916, and this unpopularity was accentuated by the knowledge that promotion of men of other classes was being retarded owing to a large proportion of the number of Indian officers and non-commissioned officers allowed in the establishment of the Battalion being held by Afridis, whose total numbers were very small in comparison. Moreover, several Afridis of influence, who had a grudge against the Battalion for one reason and another were now in Tirah. Taking everything into consideration the Commanding Officer decided it would be best to sever all connection with Afridis and to dispose of those remaining in the Battalion in the best way possible. After several months of correspondence, dating from February 1917, the military authorities in India acceded to this request, and orders were received in August 1917 to despatch all Afridis with the 58th Rifles to East Africa, where they would join the 55th Rifles. Accordingly all Afridis at Battalion Headquarters entrained for Suez on 26 August, under Subadar Anar Gul, 55th Rifles F.F., and proceeded by transport to East Africa, picking up en route those Afridis who were at Tor. It was not without regret that the officers parted with this class, which had done so well for their battalion on many occasions, but operations being now against Turks, and the Battalion on the eve of again proceeding to the front, it was considered best in the interests of the Battalion and there was undoubtedly a feeling of relief that the Afridis had been sent to another sphere of action. On 2 September C and D Companies, strength 3 British, 6 officers and 368 other ranks arrived at Ismailia having been relieved at Tor and Abu Zanima by Egyptian Army troops.

The Battalion was now under orders to proceed to the Palestine front, to join the 234th Brigade, 75th Division replacing the Royal Lancashire Fusiliers which was decimated with fever contracted in East Africa.

While at Ismailia a great deal of training had been carried out, especially in night advances, and open formations – also musketry and route marching and the Battalion was fit and well together. Pack equipment had been issued in July in place of the old bandolier equipment. Lewis guns were now issued with which no one was acquainted. The Vickers guns were taken away, much to the regret of teams, who were really very proficient. However, machine gunnery had become a specialised matter and machine gun companies had been formed from which attachments were made to units as required.

On 12 September, the Battalion left Ismailia by route march for Kantara which was now the base for operations east of the Canal. On 13 September, the Battalion arrived at Kantara and left the same day for Belah, the advance base, where it arrived on 14th and marched the same evening to a bivouac camp in the Wadi Reuben. The Battalion was now attached to the 234th Brigade, 75th Division; and was located about two miles from the front line of the troops investing Gaza. A very unfortunate event now occurred. At dawn on 16 September, two Yusufzai Pathans shot and killed another Yusufzai and, taking their rifles made off into open country before they could be stopped, and disappeared into one of the numerous nullahs with which the country was sown. After several hours of fruitless search the troops returned to camp. About 10 a.m. a platoon of Sikhs, which was carrying out some small tactical exercise near the Officers' Mess, was fired on by the two men who had deserted, and who had crept back towards the camp. In ten minutes they were rounded up, one being killed and the other severely wounded. The motive for their crime of murdering the other Yusufzai is unknown, but it is more than probable that they had made immoral proposals to their victim to which he refused to accede. It is conjectured that after committing the crime and running away, they realised that they would be unable to escape either to the front or rear, and so formed the plan to return to camp, murder any British officers they could see and sell their lives as dearly as possible. Their position when they were surrounded, within 200 yards of the Officers' Mess points to this supposition: and it is also possible that they had some false notion that they, as Mohommadans, were being led to fight against Turks, their co-religionists, and such action was improper. The fortunate accident of the Sikh platoon coming across them frustrated this plan. In the subsequent enquiry the two Yusufzai Subadars in their evidence inclined to think that the affair was one of disloyalty on the part of miscreants, and stated that they could not hold themselves responsible that another such occurrence would not happen. Under the circumstances the Divisional Commander applied for the withdrawal of all Pathans from the 58th Rifles – the Company to be replaced by a company from some other unit. This was not carried out until 23 October during which time the behaviour of the Pathans was excellent and nothing untoward occurred, although they were several times in front line trenches. It was now felt by all that the affair had been much-exaggerated: that whatever might have been the motive for the crime of the two Yusufzais on 16 September, the heart and loyalty of all the remainder was sound. Especially was this felt in regard to the Khattaks of the 55th Rifles, whose conduct had always been exemplary, and who were extremely hurt and distressed at being included in the order to remove all Pathans. Every endeavour was made to retain them: but official letters and personal reviews were unavailing: the Divisional Commander would risk no further incident which might occasion desertion to the enemy, or even worse, bring a bad name on the Division, and be a bad example for other Mohomadan troops serving in it. Such things had happened in Mesopotamia and might easily occur here. Had there not been the grave suspicion that the two Yusufzais at Wadi Reuben Camp had crept back with the intention of murdering British officers, and, above all, had the Yusufzai officers at the Court of Enquiry been able and willing to say that they would be responsible for the loyalty of all the Yusufzais, it is likely the affair would have been passed over. Doubtless it was asking a great deal of the Yusufzai officers. Recruiting had of necessity been loosely carried out: Pathan recruits sent to the Depot by recruiting officers, had to be accepted. Their antecedents and character in most cases were unknown to the officers and non-commissioned officer of their class. Both the miscreants were trans-border men and there were several others in the Company. It was a difficult and distressing matter to settle. But the Divisional Commander adhered to his first decision, and on 23 October the Pathan Company, under Lieutenant S. Gray, was sent back to be attached to the 101st Grenadiers on the Suez Canal.

A company of Punjabi Mohommadans of the 101st Grenadiers joined the Battalion for duty on 24 October. The incident was thus closed. The subsequent movements of this Company were as follows: in March 1918 the 101st Grenadiers were ordered up to Palestine and this Pathan Company was sent to join the 55th Rifles in East Africa. When that Battalion moved to India a number of Yusufzais of the 58th Rifles, who had been invalided, returned, when convalescent, to the Battalion Depot in Multan. The remainder were drafted to and formed the nucleus of the 2nd Battalion 55th Rifles which was then being raised: and of this Battalion Subadar Hamid Khan became Subadar-Major. Further enlistments of Yusufzai were carried out at the Depot in India: and in September 1918, half a company of this class, under Jemadar Ajun Khan, arrived as a reinforcement in time to take part in the last great battle in Palestine. In this battle and in their prior service in East Africa, and elsewhere, they thoroughly re-established their reputation for loyalty and courage.

To return to the Battalion in camp at Wadi Reuben. On 24 September the Battalion relieved the 1st Battalion, 4th Cornwall Light Infantry in front line posts at Mendur: ten posts in all were taken over, in all of which there should have been at least three signallers exclusive of those with Battalion Headquarters and reserve company. This made communication very difficult: but later on six British signallers were attached to Battalion Headquarters and remained with the Battalion for the rest of the campaign, which made a vast difference.

It was now that the need of trained observers was felt: a large expanse of country had to be carefully watched by men accustomed to use telescope and binoculars: every enemy movement noted and recorded at once by a second man in the observation post, and all observers reports collected at certain hours in a central intelligence office, written up carefully and passed on to the Brigade Intelligence officer. It required men highly trained in knowing what to look for – how to read a map, points of the compass, use of telescope, et cetera, et cetera. As such observers will always be required in stationary warfare it is as well to record this difficulty experienced by the Battalion at this period owing to lack of sufficient trained men.

On 29 September, the Battalion was relieved in the Mendur posts by the composite battalion of the composite force. The latter consisted of Italian Bersaglieri, French, British West Indians, Indian Imperial Service Cavalry and Infantry, and Indian Sappers and Miners. This force was irreverently known as the Golliwogs. The composite battalion was the Gwalior and Alwar Imperial Service battalions amalgamated. On 30 September the Battalion came into Brigade Reserve in the Sheikh Abbas El Mendur sector of the line: its strength being 11 British and 16 Indian officers 876 others ranks. The Battalion was chiefly engaged in burying cable by day and forming advanced ration dumps by night: this being work in connection with a future advance against the enemy. There was a great shortage of fuel and for several days biscuits had to be issued; there being no fuel to cook *atta*. Later on this occurred frequently, the country being very devoid of fuel. On 8 October about one-third of the men, who had gone on furlough to India in June last, rejoined. The remainder had been put on a ship at Bombay, which "by mistake" conveyed them to Basra! (Official Report).

On 9 October, the Battalion relieved the 2nd Battalion, 3rd Gurkhas in front line trenches on Mansura ridge, and was in turn relieved on the night 12/13 October by the 2nd Battalion 5th Hampshire Regiment– the Battalion occupying four strong posts in the second line defences. On 23 October, as recorded above, the Pathan Company under Lieutenant Gray left the Battalion and proceeded to the Base Depot at Kantara for attachment to the 101st Grenadiers; a Punjabi Mohomadan Company of the Grenadiers under Lieutenant B. Douglas strength 2 British and 4 Indian officers, 208 other ranks, joined the Battalion on 24 October in replacement of the Pathan Company. This new Company was a fine lot of men but unfortunately contained no specialists, i.e. Lewis gunners, signallers, observers and sniper scouts, nor men trained in transport duties. This was a severe handicap to the Battalion as the training of all these had to be taken in hand at once, whereas the Pathan Company had possessed the best sniper scouts and Lewis gunners in the Battalion. On 22 October a post in the front line known as 'Whale Post' was taken over from the 2nd Battalion 5th Devon Regiment.

On 30 October the remaining three companies of the Battalion took over the front line trenches on Mansura ridge from the 2nd Battalion 4th Somersets. A good deal of shelling was going on from our guns, which were cutting enemy wire and shelling his rail-head. There was not much retaliation from the enemy side, but when he did fire his shelling was extremely accurate and well placed.

On 31 October two men of B Company were wounded by shell fire.

On 1 November the area occupied by B Company was heavily shelled by enemy 5-inch howitzers which were searching for the guns of our two South African Batteries which had been covering a raid by the 3rd Battalion, 3rd Gurkhas, the night before on Outpost Hill. Most of the shells fell short of the batteries and just over B Company reserve area. Jemadar Fazal Dad was unfortunately killed and four other ranks wounded while taking cover after the first salvo. At this time our forces on the right had been attacking the Turks at Bir Saba for two days: Bir Saba had been captured but the general advance was still held up. The Battalion was in constant readiness to move at hours notice.

On 3 November at about 8.30 a.m. the enemy began to shell heavily the area around the artillery observation post close to Battalion Headquarters. The night duties were back from front line trenches in their rest area, and while hurrying forward to take up alarm posts a 5-inch shell caught a Lewis gun team of C Company (Sikhs) when just entering a trench. Four men were killed and three wounded and the Lewis gun destroyed. In the evening the enemy made a half hearted attack on the Apex post but was repulsed by the 123rd Rifles on our right: at the same time our Battalion front line and Headquarters heavily shelled for half an hour, but no casualties occurred.

In the meantime the 54th Division on the left of our line had been attacking the enemy's right with some success. On 5 November Whale Post was very heavily shelled, but no casualties resulted:

small parties of the enemy approached various parts of our line both on the right and left, but never looked like attacking.

On 6 November the battle on the right turned in our favour and the Turks were in full retreat.

On the night 6/7 November an attack was launched by our left, which got through the enemy defences. On 7 November a strong patrol under Subadar Karam Singh found the Turkish trenches opposite our centre still occupied, the patrol retired steadily under shrapnel and machine gun fire. On the night 7/8 November patrol under Lieutenant Dowland penetrated enemy trenches opposite our centre and found them unoccupied. On the night 8/9 November the Battalion was relieved by Patiala Imperial Service troops and marched to the position of concentration of the 234th Brigade.

On 10 November the Battalion advanced to Beit Hanun the old Turkish rail-head, past Gaza and the enemy trenches. It was interesting to note the havoc wrought by our guns. At one place a whole train loaded with ammunition had been blown to pieces by a lucky shot from a big naval gun. Prisoners were being brought back by hundreds, escorted by Indian cavalry. So rapid had been the advance that many of the cavalry had been without food or water for nearly sixty hours and had to return to Gaza to water. The Brigade bivouacked at Deir Sineid: no water was obtainable.

On 11 November, the Brigade advanced to just beyond Eijeh, a very hot and dusty march, a little water was obtained. On 12 November the Brigade again advanced passing through Julius and El Garbiyeh and bivouacked about two miles north of the latter village.

The 75th Division had now advanced aloud thirty miles north of Gaza and the position was as follows. The 52nd Division was on the left of the 75th Division and the ANZAC Mounted Division on its right. The enemy held a strong line behind the villages Yasur, El Kustineh and Tel Elturmis opposed by the 232nd and 233rd Brigades of the 75th Division, with the 234th Brigade in reserve. Orders were received on 12 November to push back the enemy and to advance at all costs and capture the Junction Railway Station some eight miles further north.

The ground to be won by the 75th Division was divided into three objectives: first, the villages of Yasur, EI Kustineh and Tel Elturmis, second the high ground two miles north-east of these villages – these two objectives were to be taken by the 232nd and 233rd Brigades, the 234th Brigade being in reserve. The third objective, known as the Junction Railway Station where the rail ways from the south, from Jerusalem and from Erramleh met, four miles north-east of the second objective, was to be taken by the 234th Brigade, up to then in Divisional Reserve. The attack commenced about 9.30 a.m. on 13 November and was stoutly resisted by the Turks. By 15.30 the first objective had not been attained nor had touch been achieved with the Australians on our right, and the 234th Brigade was echeloned on the right flank to protect it. At 12.15 orders were received to 'detach one company of the 58th Rifles, F.F. to protect the right flank of the 234th Brigade.' D Company (attached company of the 101st Grenadiers) under Captain R. B. Kitson, was detailed for this duty, and at 12.30 proceeded to the northern outskirts of Tel Elturmis village; where no enemy were found.

At 14.00 hours a report was received from Captain Kitson that British cavalry were operating to his front and right flank. The ground there was very undulating and much broken up with nullahs and the Company was frequently out of touch with the Battalion. At 16.55 a message brought by a runner from Captain Kitson, timed 16.15, stated briefly that the Company was involved with the enemy and required reinforcement. Just as this message was received the Australian cavalry which was operating on our right came into view and swept up into line over the ground where D Company was engaged, and a whole British battalion of the 233rd Brigade which appeared to have lost touch with its Brigade advanced over the same ground. But it was just too late. It seems that some Australian cavalry operating in front of D Company had come into touch with some enemy, entrenched behind the railway, and were driven off by machine gun fire. Whereupon Captain Kitson observing enemy movement and being apprehensive of counter-attack by the enemy, himself, ordered D Company to extend and attack.

It is conjectured that the Company being too zealous to close with the enemy had pushed on too fast and had been badly mauled by machine guns at close range. Both Captain Kitson and Lieutenant Douglas (101st Grenadiers) were killed, also 23 other ranks: three of the four Indian officers and 42 men were wounded, all of the 101st Grenadiers, except seven Lewis gunners and signallers of the 58th who were attached to this Company. The Company penetrated part of the enemy's position and nine dead Turks were counted, but, being somewhat disorganised, the Company was then withdrawn 500 yards by Subadar Ahmad Din to re-organise. It was to some extent an unfortunate affair, but there is little doubt that the enemy, whose strength was estimated at a full battalion and four machine guns, was about to launch a counter-attack, and Captain Kitson's action checked him.

Captain Kitson's loss was greatly felt. He had been in the Battalion for thirteen years. He was an excellent officer and had been unfortunate when the war broke out in having to remain with Burma Military Police, instead of accompanying his battalion to France. After completing his tour of service with British Military Police he at once rejoined the Battalion at the end of 1916. He was always very keen on coming to close quarters with the enemy, and it is feared that his keenness on this occasion was the cause of his death.

At 19.00 hours on this date the 232nd and 233rd Brigades had captured their first objectives but were still short of their second objective. It was, however, apparent that the enemy was retiring- and orders were received for the 234th Brigade to advance by night on to the third objective.

At about 22.30, the 234th Brigade advanced along the main road in column of route – the 123rd Rifles being in advance and transport bringing up the rear. No guns accompanied the column: these were to advance at daybreak. There was no attempt at surprise or quiet. Nothing occurred until the column had advanced some five miles, when the advance guard encountered the enemy about one and a half miles west of the Junction Station. After a brief encounter the enemy retired. He then attempted a counter-attack but his troops were evidently unnerved and it did not materialise. Patrols were sent out and a number of orders were now received to entrench.

At daylight it was apparent that the enemy had vacated the position and was in full retreat. Two trains were observed steaming away towards Ludd, but as no guns had yet come up nothing could be done. It was afterwards ascertained that these trains carried General Von Kress, Commanding the Turkish Forces, and his staff – had the Brigade advanced instead of entrenching, and got across the railway an immense number of important prisoners and rolling stock would probably have been secured. At 7.30 two platoons of the 123rd Rifles with some armoured cars advanced to the railway station and captured 300 prisoners. No further advance was made until 9.30 when the Brigade advanced in column down the hill towards the station. It was immediately shelled by enemy rearguard artillery. The Battalion shook out very quickly and steadily into open order and continued to advance across the railway – the 123rd Rifles being on its right. B Company cleared all to its front advancing some 1,000 yards north-east of the railway line. A Company covered the left flank, C Company being in reserve. D Company which had been left behind to collect dead and wounded after their action the day before had not yet come up. The Battalion made good its position and remained in situ awaiting orders – but none were received. As the enemy appeared to have withdrawn leaving only guns and outposts with machine guns, picquets were established and the companies withdrawn for rations and a much-needed rest. During the afternoon a party of our sappers blew up the railway bridge 500 yards north of railway station without giving any warning. As a consequence Subadar Karam Singh, and two other ranks were severely wounded by flying debris. There was no reason to blow up the bridge and it was entirely unexpected – it had to be rebuilt immediately afterwards. Our casualties during 14 November were 1 Indian officer and 7 other ranks wounded, this was very light seeing that the Battalion was under shell fire from 09.30 until 14.00 hours, and A and B Companies under machine gun fire most of the day.

At 9.30 on 15 November the enemy again shelled our position and our guns replied. It was noticed that a forward move by the 123rd Rifles was in progress and, as no orders had been received for over forty-eight hours from the 234th Brigade Headquarters, the 58th immediately advanced on to the ridge 2,000 yards north-east of the railway; covering the left of the 123rd Rifles. The ridge was captured after a short fight with loss of only 2 men killed – 22 prisoners, 25 rifles and a machine gun were captured. Battalion Headquarters were established on the position won and outposts pushed forward, a portion of the 233rd Brigade being now on our left. This part of the line was taken over on 16 November by the 123rd Rifles and the Battalion moved 1,500 yards north, connecting with the 52nd Division. It remained here until the evening of 18 November when orders were received that the 75th Division would advance, with the city of Jerusalem as its objective. A special role was allotted to the 58th Rifles: to piquet the pass north-east of Latrun, and the Battalion was to be attached for this purpose to the 232nd Brigade, which it was to join on the morning of 19 November at Latrun.

This involved a march of eight miles across our own front to Latrun and a further two miles to where the hills began to close in on the road and the precautions of hill warfare became necessary. During the night of the 18/19 November all superfluous kit, including packs, had been sent back, according to orders, to the Junction Railway Station: a number of men were away as unloading party for this purpose: and the night had been very short and disturbed in consequence of frequent orders which came in. At dawn on 19 November, no rations had arrived and transport was all absent. The Battalion waited for rations until 06.00 hours but as, even then, it was late moving off to get into its position, it was impossible to remain any longer. At 10.00, the Battalion managed to reach Latrun, having forced its way past columns of infantry, artillery and transport train marching in the same direction. An hour's rest was imperative. About 11.30 hours the head of the Battalion had reached the pass to Jerusalem: a few shells had been fired by the enemy (see map V).

The latest information from 75th Division headquarters at Latrun, from cavalry covering the front as far as the Latrun pass, was that

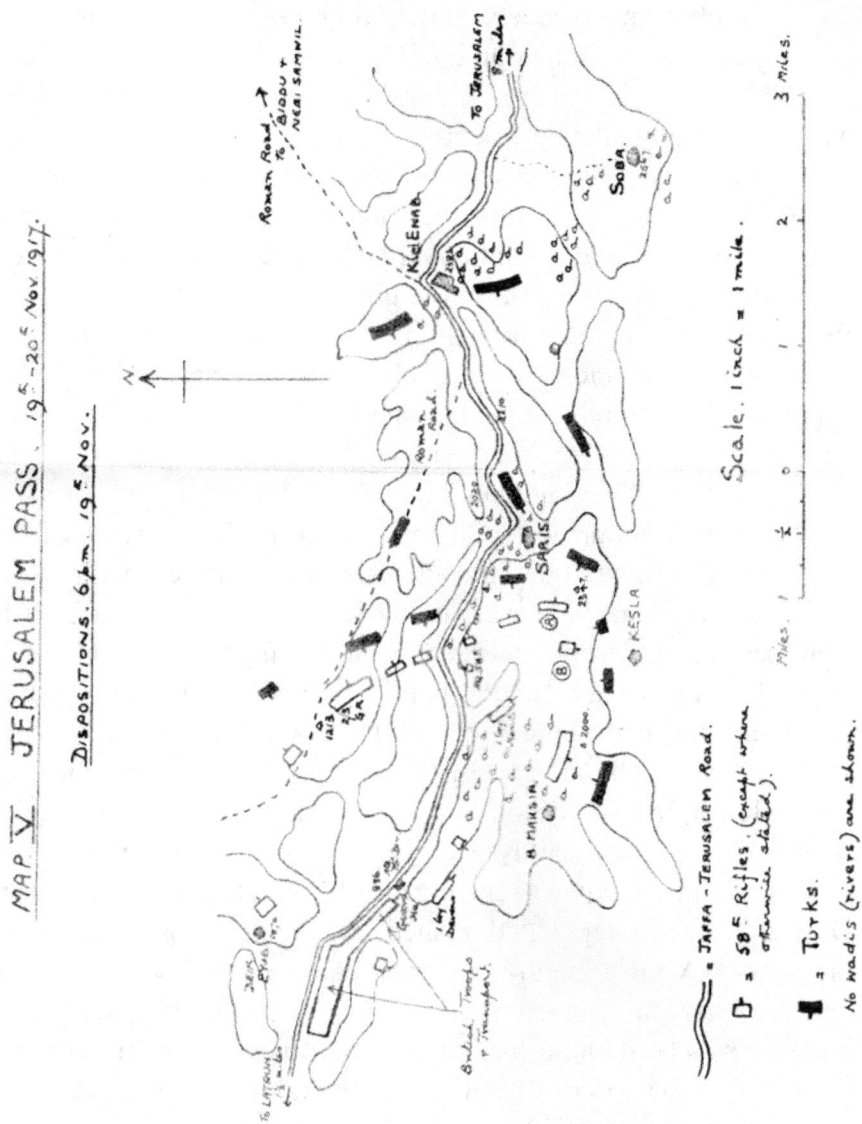

very few enemy were to be seen and that only slight opposition might be expected. The first two picquets occupied their positions without incident. The next, on the left, came under heavy fire and was unable to advance. Very heavy rifle and machine gun fire was now opened by the enemy and the road also, was shelled. It became necessary to send a company upon each flank to clear up the situation. D Company under Lieutenant Farley advanced up a steep wooded hill on the right and occupied it without much opposition but its advance was held up by machine gun fire from the village of Beit Mahsir and neighbouring hamlets. C Company under Major Waller on the left was also held up under heavy fire: half of A Company was sent to reinforce it, and the advance continued slowly. It was evident by now that the enemy were fresh and determined troops and intended resistance. At 13.45 a company of the 2nd Battalion 3rd Gurkhas reinforced our left flank and half a company of the 1st Battalion 5th Devon Regiment went up to the right flank, and both our companies were able to advance slightly. With this security, although the country quite blind, the hills on either flank being very steep, high and wooded, the remaining one and a half companies of the Battalion under the Commanding Officer felt their way forward. Towards dusk about two miles of road from the entrance of the pass had been secured and the advance guard had reached a small mosque about one mile west of Saris village. The last picquets were sent up in a very uncertain light, leaving only two platoons in the Commanding Officer's hand as a reserve. The enemy had blown up the road about every 200 yards for a width of twenty yards or more. The men had marched ten miles and fought over two miles of ground without rest except for one hour at midday. It now began to rain heavily and was very cold. During the night one of the last picquets sent out on the night, under Lieutenant Dowland, encountered and rushed two enemy posts, capturing prisoners. A third enemy post was captured at dawn and more prisoners taken. Lieutenant Dowland's action, with only one platoon, was bold and effective, and an important position on our right flank was captured and held. He was joined after dark by two platoons of the 2nd Battalion, 5th Hampshire Battalion which gave him considerable moral support until recalled to their own unit at daylight on 20 November. The last picquet sent up was also to the right flank under Subadar Mohommad Arabi Khun, I.O.M. He felt his way in the dark and rain to the top of the hill overlooking Saris village. At dawn, recognising this to be a most important position and having only a platoon with him, he sent back for ammunition and reinforcements, which were sent up to him. A small enemy picquet was driven back and his patrols reported Saris strongly held by enemy. At 08.00 on the morning of 20 November the enemy endeavoured to recapture this point, but were repulsed. They now shelled the hill and again attacked, only to be repulsed. The enemy heavily shelled the Subadar's position; 2 men were killed and 9 wounded. At this moment two platoons of the 2nd Battalion 5th Hampshire Regiment were moving up the hill to his right and the Subadar called on them for assistance.

At least two companies of the enemy now attacked the Subadar's position and were again driven back. Seeing that our troops were attacking Saris village from the north side, Subadar Mohommad Arabi counter-attacked the enemy, and with the two British platoons, drove them back on Saris village and into the arms of the Somerset Light Infantry, to whom they surrendered. Subadar Mohommad Arabi showed great initiative and determination in this action, and was suitably rewarded with the 1st Class of the Order of Merit, a high distinction. He was ably assisted by Subadar Lal Khan and Havildar Wali Dad, both 55th Rifles F.F., attached. In the meantime C Company on the left had pushed back the enemy and made good that flank.

Early on the morning of 20 November the 232nd Brigade Commander having come up, the situation was explained to him. The Battalion was ordered to hold on to its positions and the 232nd Brigade pushed on to attack Kuriyat El Enab which it captured at about 15.00 hours.

The pass was now full of troops and transport. There had been heavy rain and it was still raining. Companies had been out on the hills without food or warm clothing for over twenty-four hours and the men were exhausted. Casualties, however, had been light, 1 British officer wounded, 6 other ranks killed and 34 wounded. All the latter were safely brought in and evacuated.

After Enab had been captured the Battalion was ordered to concentrate and advance to that village. Having obtained rations, the Battalion proceeded at 21.30 along a road blocked by transport, arriving at Enab at 01.00 hours on 21 November and bivouacked in liquid mud.

The Battalion remained attached to the 232nd Brigade and was now ordered to occupy a small village named Soba, perched on the crest of an isolated hill on the right (south) side of the Jerusalem road: here it covered the right flank of the Division. The village was occupied without opposition. Meantime the 233rd and 234th Brigades had proceeded north-east along the old Roman road their object being the capture of Nebi Samwil, the key position of Jerusalem, and to cut the enemy line of communications from the city to the north: also to capture El Jib and Bir Nabala villages.

The Battalion remained at Soba until 24 November. There was excellent spring water to be had, a few vegetables were obtainable but little else. For four days, from 19th to 22nd, the men had been on less than half rations and entirely living on biscuits: no *atta* was obtainable. A 1lb tin of condensed milk had to be apportioned to twelve men and no meat or tobacco had been seen for a week. Things began to improve, however, directly the road from Latrun had been repaired and guns and ammunition had come through. The men were very cheerful from knowing that they had acquitted themselves well in the fighting up-to-date and especially in the fight for the Pass. Moreover we were in sight of the city of Jerusalem. The fight for El Jib, Bir Nabala and Neby Samwil continued day and night, the 233rd and 234th Brigades being involved: they captured their objectives but were heavily counter-attacked and suffered severe losses, but held on to most of what they had won. The Turks had evidently been reinforced with first-line troops and numerous guns and were offering a strenuous opposition to the capture.

On 24 November the 60th (London) Division was brought up, to take out the 75th Division, which, owing to heavy casualties, could make no further progress.

The Battalion was relieved at Soba by the 13th London Battalion on the afternoon of 24 November, and directed to march to Kubeilbeh and rejoin the 234th Brigade. On arrival there it came into Divisional Reserve: but as the 60th Division was already relieving the 75th Division, the Battalion was directed to remove back to Kuriyat El Eualb, where it arrived at 23.30 hours on 24 November.

That the 75th Division only just failed to capture Jerusalem was a matter for keen regret by all ranks. It had come up against an unexpected strong resistance, and was without support by heavy artillery. However, the Division took and held Nebi Samwil, the key of the position, and handed it over to the 60th Division, which, fresh and well fed and having suffered few casualties since the fighting began at the end of October, and being shortly afterwards supported by heavy artillery, entered the city, with no opposition two weeks later.

On 26 November, 234th Brigade moved to Junction Station and on 27th to Beshitt where it went into camp for rest and refitting. The following officers, together with a small draft from India, joined on the 26 November: Captain H. C. Laird (101st Grenadiers), Lieut J. Mckay (I.A.R.O.), 2nd Lieutenant P. P. Abernethy and Subadar Tikka Khan.

Casualties in the Battalion during November were 2 British officers, 1 Indian officer and 36 other ranks killed: 1 British officer, 4 Indian officers and 95 other ranks wounded.

The following immediate rewards were gained during the month. Subadar Ahmad Din, 101st Grenadiers, (attached) the Indian Distinguished Service Medal, for his steady and skilful withdrawal and reorganisation of D Company, of which he was in command after Captain Kitson and Lieutenant Douglas had been killed in the flank guard action on 13 November.

No. 1873 Naik Mohammad Yusuf, No. 1177 Lance-Naik Gaur Ali, No. 1893 Sepoy Mohommad Khan and No. 4000 Sepoy Mohammad Khan, all of the 101st Grenadiers (attached) for gallantry and good leadership in the same action, received the Indian Distinguished Service Medal.

Captain Kitson was also mentioned in despatches, and his prompt action commended in appreciating the situation and attacking the enemy before their counter-attack could develop.

Captain G. R. Dowland was awarded the Military Cross for his initiative and dash in capturing three enemy posts on the night 19/20 November and taking a number of prisoners, and thus securing a portion of our right flank during critical hours of dark and daybreak. In this action he received especially able support from No. 3346 Havildar Fazal Dad and No. 3885 Lance-Naik Rahim Ali, who were awarded the Indian Distinguished Service Medal.

Subadar Mohommad Arabi Khan, I.O.M. (2nd Class) was awarded the 1st Class of the same order for his skilful leadership in seizing a most important tactical point on our right front and gallantry in holding the same for several hours against repeated enemy counter-attacks. In this he was most ably assisted by Subadar Lal Khan, 55th Rifles F.F. (attached) who was awarded the 2nd Class Indian Order of Merit and by No. 1841 Havildar Wali Dad 55th Rifles F.F. (attached) who was mentioned in despatches. Others who were mentioned for gallant conduct were No. 3329 Havildar Mokarrab Khan and No. 3851 Lance-Naik Tikka Khan, 55th Rifles, who brought up ammunition to Subadar Mohammad Arabi Khan's position under heavy shell fire, and No. 3914 Sepoy Mehar Khan and No. 3708 Sepoy Itbar Khan both of the 55th Rifles who rescued a severely wounded comrade exposed to heavy fire.

On 1 December the 234th Brigade moved to Yebna and camped on the sand about one mile from the sea. It remained here until 7 December and the men were able to indulge in sea bathing which was much appreciated. During this time warm clothing and new boots were issued but no greatcoats were available.

On 6 December Major A. A. Smith, rejoined the Battalion having left the Depot at Multan on 23 November; a record in rapidity, as movement of individuals was much hampered at this time. Subadar-Major Tikka Khan was now despatched towards Jerusalem with an escort of fifty rank and file, to do duty over the Mohommadan holy places of that city, which was expected to surrender immediately. Our troops entered Jerusalem on 9 December.

It is worth recording here an incident which happened while our troops were on duty over the famous Mosque of Omar, one of the most revered of the Mohommadan holy places. The head Sheikh of this mosque, a man noted for his learning and integrity, was conversing with Subadar-Major Tikka Khan, who questioned him concerning the consumption of the tinned meat ration by Mohommadans – certain of whom had refused it on account of uncertainty as to whether the contents were lawful food, as the meat might not have been killed in the orthodox manner. The Sheikh assured him that under stress of circumstances not only was the meat lawful but it was incumbent on soldiers to eat it to maintain the strength necessary to carry out the duties which they had sworn to perform. As halal meat was almost impossible to obtain at that time the Sheikh was asked if he would himself eat a portion of the tinned meat ration, to which he promptly replied that a tin should be brought and opened. This was done and the Sheikh and Subadar-Major ate the contents in the presence of a number of sepoys. During the whole of the operations in November there had been great difficulty in obtaining water and *atta*.

It was quite impossible to observe religious scruples with the former, and biscuits had constantly to be eaten in lieu of chapattis. There was no transport available to make separate storage of water possible, and all water was poured into the single 600 gallon canvas trough which was carried for this purpose. A compromise was made by which the trough was divided in the middle, the Sikhs and Dogras using one end and the Mohommadans the other. The stress of circumstances and the good example set by the officers and higher caste men soon did away with any prejudices in the minds of the more obstinate men.

On 7 December the 234th Brigade moved, in torrents of rain, two miles across country to Kubeibeh where it remained until 10 December during which time rain was almost incessant, night and day, and the cold was great. The want of greatcoats was much felt, and the small bivouac sheets fixed to 2' 6" poles was the only tentage available.

On 10 December the Battalion received orders to march independently to Jimsu and join the 232nd Brigade. Its strength was 11 British and 12 Indian officers, and 697 other ranks. It must be remembered that all this time the Battalion was not a permanent unit of the 75th Division: it had only been lent pending the arrival from India of the 2nd Battalion 4th Devon Regiment, which was to replace the Battalion of the Lancashire Fusiliers, which had suffered so severely from Malaria in East Africa that it was unable to accompany the 234th Brigade when that Brigade moved up to Gaza in September 1917. The 2nd Battalion 4th Devons was now about to join the 234th Brigade and the 58th Rifles was, therefore, surplus in the 75th Division and was employed by the Divisional Commander as expedient. From some points of view this was unsatisfactory, but it resulted in the Battalion being sent where any fighting was in progress, which was a source of much gratification.

On 10 December therefore, the Battalion marched to 232nd Brigade headquarters near Jimsu, across a roadless, rain sodden country and went into bivouac with the anticipation of going into action the next day.

On 11 December C Company (Sikhs), under Major A. A. Smith, supported a company of the 1st Battalion 4th Devons in capturing the Khurbat Zebdah ridge; afterwards passing through the Devons and capturing Khurbat Hamid, a commanding point, after a short fight in which 1 man was killed and 2 wounded. In the evening the whole ridge was taken over by A and B Companies, C and D companies being kept in reserve.

In the meantime, the 2nd Battalion 3rd Gurkhas on our left had captured Budras village, in which action their right flank was covered by A Company (Dogras and P.M.s) under Lieutenant R.

G. Ekin: this Company put a Turkish machine gun out of action and captured very cleverly a Turkish officer and ten men.

On 13 December the Khurbat Zebdah ridge was handed over to the 123rd Rifles and on 14th the Battalion moved to Budras to take part in an attack on the Khurbat Ibanneh ridge.

This took place early on 15 December, the Battalion being on the left of the 232nd Brigade and connecting with the 2nd Battalion 5th Hampshire Regiment of the 163rd Brigade, 54th Division, on its left. The ridge was very steep but the Battalion climbed the 600 feet in splendid style and in faultless formation: true, the opposition was slight owing to the magnificent shooting of the South African Brigade of Field Artillery which completely put the enemy machine guns out of action. The Battalion was in fine form and if allowed to go on would have carried all before it. Two officers and eleven men of the enemy were captured, and a machine gun.

In the above action the following were particularly brought to notice: Subadar Kehr Singh, who, with his platoon, on 15 December, drove the retiring enemy off a commanding position 1,000 yards in front of our final objective on which they were reforming to enfilade a salient in our line. No. 3374 Naik Dewa Singh and No. 2937 Lance-Naik Bhag Singh who, on 15 December, went out nearly three-quarters of a mile to their front and under rifle and machine gun fire both going and returning, brought in No. 4127 Sepoy Man Singh, who had been wounded and unavoidably left by a retiring patrol. Lance-Naik Bhag Singh was himself wounded during the return journey.

Naik Dewa Singh was awarded a bar to the Indian Distinguished Service Medal he had gained in France, and Lance-Naik Bhag Singh was awarded the Indian Distinguished Service Medal.

No. 1226 Sepoy Umar Khan and No. 1968 Sepoy Dilbar Shah both of the 101st Grenadiers, attached, who, in the action on 15 December, were prominent in following up an enemy machine gun detachment, capturing the gun and taking prisoners. Both were awarded the Indian Distinguished Service Medal.

Our casualties from 1 to 16 December were 3 other ranks killed and 12 wounded.

On 17 December the following joined the Battalion: Captain A.I. G. McConkey from hospital, Lieutenant D. S. Gillespie, Lieutenant C. R. Spear, 1 Indian officer and 90 other ranks from the Depot in India: 2 Indian officers and 74 other ranks from the 101st Grenadiers.

On 18 December our position on Khurbat Ibanneh was taken over by the 2nd Battalion 3rd Gurkhas and the Battalion moved to Beit Nabala and became support to the troops on Khurbat Bornat, a weak point in the line and held by the 163rd Brigade, 54th Division; and in course of being taken over by the 232nd Brigade. The Battalion bivouacked in an olive grove under waterproof sheets and in caves under the hill known as Khurbat Zefizfiheh. Working parties were sent nightly to help in the consolidation of Khurbat Bornat, held by the 2nd Battalion 4th Somerset Light Infantry which was receiving a good deal of attention from enemy guns. Rain was incessant, roads practically nonexistent and rations had to be brought up on camels from four miles to the rear of the line, the camels had frequently to cross nullahs in spate. However, the rations were not very good, there was a liberal issue of rum and the men were well content.

On 22 December our line was moved slightly forward to straighten it. No opposition was encountered. Two companies under Lieutenant Ekin occupied the ground taken and were relieved next day by the 1st Battalion 4th Devons.

During the month of December 1917 the Battalion had attacked over a front of four miles of country, had suffered casualties 4 killed and 18 wounded, and captured 28 prisoners, including three officers, and a machine gun. Christmas was extremely wet, but this did not damp the spirits of the men.

On 30 December a number of the aforementioned immediate rewards for gallant and distinguished conduct during operations, which had taken place since the advance from Gaza, were made on parade by Brigadier-General C. McLean, D.S.O., commanding the 284th Infantry Brigade.

CHAPTER V
Palestine, 1918

The Battalion remained at Beit Nabala in reserve to the 233rd Brigade until 11 January 1918, when it moved to camp at Haditheh and came into Divisional Reserve.

For the past three weeks the weather had been vile, the men had only waterproof sheets as shelters, and they and the horse transport had a most uncomfortable time, but there was practically no sickness.

During the latter period, that is from Christmas 1917 onwards, the Battalion was chiefly engaged in road making from Deir Turif to Et Tireh, the country being entirely without lateral communications.

The following joined the Battalion at this time: Lieutenant B. C. Taylor and Lieutenant S. L. Storrow, both of the 54th Sikhs F.F. on 2 January 1918. On 13 January, Captain Holgate, I.M.S., left the Battalion to take up duties at No. 5 Indian General Hospital, Suez; and was replaced by Lieutenant P. N. Dogra, I.M.S. On 18 January the Battalion moved to a camp near Ludd and came into Corps Reserve.

On 31 January, Major R. de W. Waller, who had been wounded in the Latrun Pass on 19 November 1917, rejoined the Battalion, bringing with him a reinforcement of 63 other ranks. The strength of the Battalion on this date being 13 British, 17 Indian officers, 987 other ranks: there were also 7 British signallers and 27 Indian drivers attached.

On 2 February a detachment of 1 Indian officer and 50 other ranks of the company of the 101st Grenadiers (attached) was sent to Jerusalem to relieve the detachment under Subadar-Major Tikka Khan: the latter rejoined the Battalion on 7 February.

At this time Jemadar Madat Khan and 75 other ranks joined as a reinforcement, most of this draft came from the Depot in India. The strength of the Battalion was now 18 Indian officers and 1,058 other ranks, which included 4 Indian officers and 211 other ranks of the 101st Grenadiers. It was known that the latter were soon to be withdrawn to join their own unit which was being brought up to the front. It was also strongly rumoured that the military authorities in India were sending a new company of the 98th Infantry consisting of Hindustani Rajputs and Ahirs, as a reinforcement to the 58th Rifles F.F. in place of the(P.M.) company of the 101st Grenadiers. In view of an early resumption of hostilities, such a reinforcement of untrained men, inexperienced and without specialists, and of a race totally different from that of men of the Battalion, could not but be regarded with apprehension. Great efforts were made for permission to form a company from our own men, but sanction was not given. The Battalion, also, was in Corps Reserve, and, as the 2nd Battalion 4th Devon Regiment had replaced it in the 234th Brigade, it was a surplus battalion in the 75th Division and, as such, was threatened with becoming a Working or Pioneer Battalion. It had (as usual) done excellent work in road construction. Indeed, in conjunction with other battalions of the Division, it had done nothing but road construction since the commencement of 1918. But, whereas battalions which definitely belonged to brigades took their place in front line defences after a tour of duty in Divisional Reserve (which meant road construction) and were able to carry out some musketry and training while at the front, this Battalion, having no fixed Brigade, was incessantly employed in road making, and no opportunity for training musketry was afforded to it: only specialists, i.e., signallers, Lewis gunners and observers being excused from these working parties.

The Battalion remained in the vicinity of Ludd until 11 February, when it was ordered to relieve the 1st Battalion 5th Somerset

Light Infantry near Haditheh, and came into 75th Divisional Reserve. Road construction continued, but by 20 February this had made such progress that smaller parties were demanded, and it became possible to strike one company off duty for two days at a time for training: a range was made for Lewis gunners and snipers, and the training of 'observer-scouts' intensified. Baths and arrangements for the disinfection of clothing (known as the liceum) had been erected in the vicinity: clothing was disinfected, cleaned and renewed and all ranks inoculated against cholera and enteric. Plans for a forward move were evidently well-matured. An issue of steel helmets was made. The Sikhs, though willing to wear these, found it impossible, owing to the shallowness of the helmet, unless they let their hair fall down their backs: this plan was not adopted and, much to their relief, they were allowed to retain their *pagris*. The Dogras took to the helmet readily. A few Mussulmans objected to wearing a head-dress with a brim, as this might just prevent them placing their foreheads on the ground in time to escape eternal damnation should the end of the world suddenly come to pass. However, this objection was overruled.

On 3 March, Lieutenant P. Snell, 1st Battalion 4th Devon Regiment, joined the Battalion on appointment to the Indian Army.

On 8 March, 1 Indian officer and 50 other ranks of the 101st Grenadiers rejoined from duty at Jerusalem and, on the same date, Lieutenant A. C. Beynon, 98th Infantry joined for duty, a company of his battalion being now at Suez and on its way to join the 58th Rifles.

On 10 March, the Battalion rejoined the 234th Brigade. Headquarters and half the Battalion moved to Bireh, and the half Battalion under Major A. A. Smith to Et Tireh. The 234th Brigade was to take part in an advance on 12 March, and the role of this Battalion was to construct temporary roads and communications in rear of the fighting troops for the rapid passage of guns and supplies.

On 12 March, the advance took place and penetrated the enemy's front for a depth of three and a half miles on a front of three miles.

The Battalion carried out its duties of road construction with much success. The artillery was able to take up forward positions directly the moment came, ammunition was easily brought up, and by 15.00 hours Brigade transport and ration carts were able to reach their locations, and front line troops received rations the same evening. From 13 to 18 March the new line was being consolidated and the Battalion was engaged daily in heavy road work.

Orders were now received that the Battalion was to be again placed in the front line.

During the above period much hard and useful work had been put in, the country being very steep and precipitous. That the work done by the Battalion was much appreciated by the fighting troops, will be seen from the complimentary order (Appendix E).

On 18 March the company of the 101st Grenadiers left to rejoin their own battalion. This fine company of Punjabi Mohommadans had done most excellent work during its five months attachment to the 58th Rifles F.F., and no better troops could have replaced the Pathan Company which was sent back so unfortunately by the 75th Divisional Commander in October 1917. The company of the 101st Grenadiers was most ably commanded by Captain H. C. Laird and the senior Indian officer, Subadar Ahmad Khan was a man whose steadiness of character and courage were highly valued. Both these officers gained high honours in later operations, and both admitted having gained valuable experience during their attachment to the 58th Rifles. This Company gained seven Distinguished Service Medals while attached to this Battalion.

On 18 March the Battalion joined the 233rd Brigade at Abud. The same night two companies under Major A. A. Smith advanced and captured the village of Deir Gussaneh and the Sheikh Kauwash Ridge, little opposition was met and the position was consolidated by dawn. Headquarters and the other half Battalion advanced to a more favourable position in close support.

On 21 March a reinforcement of 1 British officer (Captain D. Montford) 3 Indian officers and 203 other ranks of the 98th Infantry joined the Battalion. This Company consisted of about one-third Rajputs of Eastern Rajputana and two-thirds Ahirs from Delhi, Hissar and Gurgaon. Seventy-five percent were recruits of some four to six months' service, their non-commissioned officers largely old men or quite new promotions. The Company was almost untrained: twenty-five percent had fired a hurried recruits' course: there was only one specialist – a signaller. Their physique was good on the whole. The Company, especially the Rajputs, at once showed many caste prejudices and objected to the order to consume biscuits as an iron ration, and also to eating food while wearing leather equipment.

It was now a question whether or not to break up the Company, and distribute it amongst the three companies of the Battalion or to leave it as a separate company, completing it with Lewis gunners, signallers and observers from effectives in the 58th Rifles F.F. For several reasons, but chiefly on account of the caste prejudices of the Ahirs and Rajputs and the possibility of their affecting our own men, it was decided to follow the latter course.

The Battalion was now on the extreme right flank of the 75th Division, connecting with the 3rd Battalion 3rd Gurkhas on the left, and the 6th Battalion, Leinster Regiment (10th Division) some distance away to the right.

The Sheikh Kauwash Ridge which had been so easily occupied by us gave an excellent field for observation. To the left front, and on the front slope of a lower ridge, named Sheikh Nafukh, was a strongly built village called El Kefr. The ground on the north (enemy's) side of this village was steep and gave good cover to the enemy, and the village itself was occupied by a few enemy with machine guns, who made things very unpleasant for the right flank of the 3rd Battalion 3rd Gurkhas, which they enfiladed.

On 22 March a strong patrol of two platoons of A Company was sent to test the defences of El Kefr, and met with strong resistance. The patrol was heavily shelled and machine gunned, and lost 2 killed and 7 wounded.

It was obvious that El Kefr was strongly held and well organised, and the patrol noticed the presence of German troops in the village.

The patrol was skilfully withdrawn by Jemadar Mirza Khan, 55th Rifles F.F. The killed and wounded and all equipment and rifles were brought in.

On 27 March orders were received to occupy a hill some 250 yards on the south-west (our own) side of El Kefr village; this hill commanded El Kefr village but was itself commanded from the Sheikh Nafukh Ridge some 500 yards distant (map VI).

This operation was skilfully carried out on the night of 27/28 March by C Company (Sikhs) under Major Waller and Captain Gillespie. The hill (afterwards called El Kefr Hill) was occupied by a few enemy who fled. The enemy immediately put down a heavy barrage of shell on this hill and in the valley between it and Sheikh Kauwash Ridge, (named the Wadi Ballut) and heavy machine gun fire was opened from the village. However, the position was held against some rather feeble counter-attacks and was consolidated.

Casualties were 4 killed and 11 wounded. The climb from the Wadi Ballut to the top of El Kefr Hill was some 500 feet and very steep.

At dawn it was apparent that cover on the hill was very scanty and there was no room for more than two platoons. Any movement was at once detected from the Sheikh Nafukh Ridge and drew artillery and machine gun fire. From close observation it

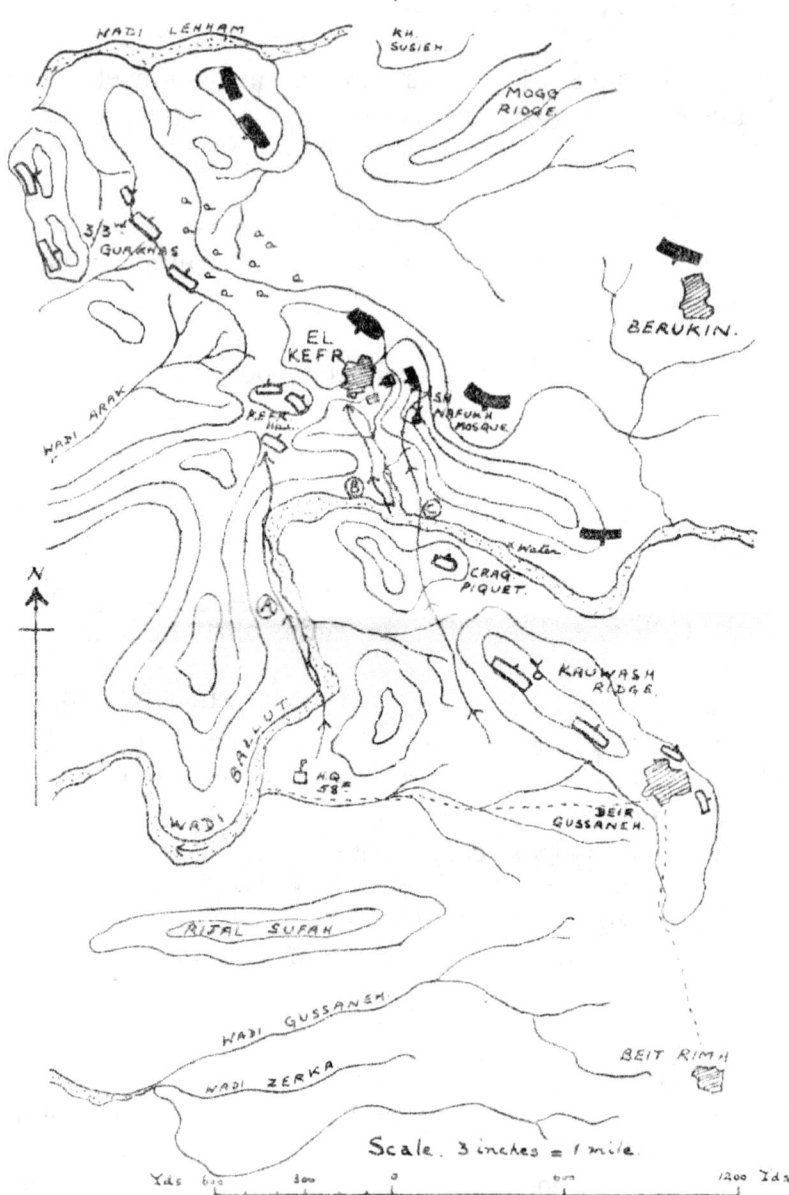

was obvious that the enemy's position was of considerable strength and organised by German officers, and the machine guns in the village were manned by Germans. The object of occupying El Kefr Hill was not apparent, as it did not in any way lessen the exposure of the right flank of the 3rd Battalion 3rd Gurkhas to enfilade fire from the hidden ground to the north of the Sheikh Nafukh Ridge. However, orders were received to hold El Kefr Hill.

On 29 March verbal orders were received from the 233rd Brigade headquarters to capture and hold El Kefr village. This also necessitated the capture of the Sheikh Nafukh Ridge, without which El Kefr could not be held. The situation was pointed out to Brigade headquarters vizt: that the Battalion was already holding a long front from Gussaneh village to El Kefr Hill, both inclusive: and that at most five platoons could be spared for the intended operation, leaving only a weak company in reserve in case of emergency; that El Kefr village was strongly held by machine guns manned by German troops and that it was more than probable that the enemy held strong reserves in Berukin village, some two miles distant. However, the 75th Division headquarters directed that the order should hold good.

It was, therefore, decided to approach the position under cover of darkness and to push in the assault at dawn.

The general scheme was for two platoons of the attached company of the 98th Infantry to seize the Nafukh ridge and secure the right flank. The signal that this had been done was to be the firing of a green very light, by the officer commanding the two platoons. Two platoons of the 58th Rifles, who would then be in position in the re-entrant from the Wadi Ballut to El Kefr village, on seeing the signal would push up the re-entrant and assault the village, assisted by one of the two platoons on El Kefr Hill. The other platoon on this point securing the left flank, and being a point on which to retire should the attack fail. The company of the 98th Infantry had asked for an opportunity to show what it could do, and so was given this chance.

At 04.45 hours on 30 March, the right flank party, two platoons 98th Infantry, having reached its objective without opposition, put up a green very light.

At 05.15 hours heavy firing and bombing broke out in El Kefr village and at 05.40 hours our artillery observation officer reported machine guns and a number of enemy on Sheikh Nafukh Ridge. Shortly after this Lieutenant Hills, in command on El Kefr Hill, reported that he had led one platoon, as arranged to cooperate in the attack on the village, but had been heavily fired on by machine guns and infantry from the village and the ridge, and that most of his platoon was out of action: that El Kefr village was full of enemy and that the two platoons of the 58th which had formed the centre attack had reached and penetrated the village, but had been attacked from the right flank and were unable to extricate themselves, No report was received from the right flank party and nothing was seen of it. C Company, in reserve, was sent up to reinforce, and the Brigade Commander was informed of the situation, and was requested to send up reinforcements.

It was apparent now that the right flank had never been secured. Small parties of two to four men of this half company were seen coming down the ridge and dribbling back towards Headquarters, and no resistance was being offered to the enemy. At 06.15 hours the enemy made a counter-attack on El Kefr Hill but was driven back by the platoon in occupation and by our supporting artillery. Two platoons from C Company were sent to El Kefr Hill with orders to hold it at all costs, as it was evident that the enemy intended to counter-attack in force. At 07.00 hours large numbers of enemy endeavoured to cross the Sheikh Nafukh Ridge to attack El Kefr Hill, but were driven back by our supporting artillery which was admirably directed by the Forward Observation Officer, Lieutenant N. J. Chamberlain, B Battery, 172nd Brigade R.F.A. The enemy continued his efforts to reach El Kefr Hill from the west of the village, but was each time repulsed. About 09.00 hours the fighting had ceased except that the enemy was barraging the Wadi Ballut with howitzers, and keeping up an accurate fire on El Kefr Hill.

At 10.00 hours two companies of the 1st Battalion, 4th Wiltshire Regiment arrived, but as the enemy had, apparently, had enough to keep him quiet, nothing was required of them.

Lieutenant A. C. Beynon of the 98th Infantry had now arrived, having been ordered back by Major A. A. Smith who was directing the centre attack. It was learned from him that on arrival of his half company at the Sheikh Nafukh mosque before dawn, Captain D. Montford, who was commanding the right flank party, had ordered him to remain there with two sections, while Captain Montford took one platoon forward. It seems that the other sections under Subadar Hindpal Singh had become detached in the darkness and were not to be found. Apparently the two sections under Lieutenant Beynon did not picquet the top of the ridge just above the mosque, and were attacked from there at 05.20 hours by enemy who did not advance on them, but kept them pinned down under fire. Lieutenant Beynon related how the men of his two sections 'melted away' (sic) by twos and threes, until, finding himself nearly alone, he too, went back and found the other two sections under Subadar Hindpal Singh, halfway up the ridge, and lying down under cover and doing nothing. With these he again advanced and tried to establish communication with his Company Commander, but owing to heavy fire from the village and the ridge above him, he was not able to get along. Again, he states the men under him began to move back in small parties and he was left with barely half a dozen men. It was now that Major Smith, learning how he was situated, ordered him to come back. What happened to Captain Montford is not and never will be known. Most of the men of his platoon came back unwounded, and all they could say was that on arrival at the top of the ridge they had been attacked, that Captain Montford had been wounded and had ordered them to retire, which they did. Nothing has ever been seen or heard since of Captain Montford: except that two weeks later an Arab reported that he had seen a number of prisoners of war wearing green putties being marched northwards, and amongst them an officer, also wearing green putties and riding a pony.

This operation then failed: and the failure must be attributed to the collapse of the right flank party. This party reached its objective unopposed and signalled that it was there, thus bringing the centre attack up a re-entrant a dangerous operation unless reasonably certain that both flanks were secure. This right flank party appears to have made but made no attempt to hold the Sheikh Nafukh Ridge, but collapsed directly the enemy opposed it. All the Indian officers and most of the non-commissioned officers and men returned unwounded, many being without their rifles and equipment which points to entire demoralisation. In the light of subsequent information, and from the strength the enemy developed on the ridge, it is doubtful if the best could have held the ridge unless heavily reinforced. But to offer no opposition when attacked was conduct as unlooked for and incomprehensible as it was disastrous: and it was bitterly resented by the men of the Battalion who suffered such heavy casualties in consequence. The Punjabi Mohommadans of the 55th Rifles F.F., attached to the 58th Rifles F.F., suffered the greatest losses [as] they formed the central attack. They were led with great élan by Lieutenant J. McKay and Subadar Lal Khan, I.O.M., whose body was found some days after inside the village: as also were the bodies of several others of this fine half company, lying together with corpses of dead enemy both Germans and Turks in and beyond the village too.

Lieutenant J. McKay was killed close to the village his orderly's body being found just by him. Jemadar Mirza Khan was wounded early in the action. Of other ranks 12 were killed, 34 missing (mostly killed) and 63 wounded. The Turkish soldiers and Arab villagers killed our wounded Dogras, but allowed wounded Mohommadans to go, after stripping them of their boots and clothing and valuables.

For the rest, it was now apparent to Divisional Headquarters that previous reports sent in from the Battalion Intelligence Officer that El Kefr village was strongly occupied and organised for defence by European troops were substantially true, and that it would require something more than five platoons, supported by a field battery of artillery, to gain this objective. Indeed, a few days later, it took a full battalion, supported by heavy howitzers, to capture the village and ridge, which was held with difficulty until operations further to the east relieved the pressure. The two

Dogra platoons of A Company which had held El Kefr Hill so gallantly and been badly mauled in the assault on the village, were relieved at dusk by a half company of B from Gussaneh village.

Lieutenant G. G. Hills who had so ably commanded them was recommended for, and received, the Military Cross.

On 31 March the enemy endeavoured to capture the observation post on the lower (north) slope of Sheikh Kauwash and the same night attempted a bombing raid on El Kefr Hill. These attacks were easily repulsed by B Company. For the next few days minor attacks on El Kefr Hill and Sheikh Kauwash were made by the enemy under machine gun barrages, and both places were frequently shelled by medium howitzers. We suffered a few casualties but easily held our positions.

On 1 April half a battalion of the 1st Battalion, 4th Wiltshire Regiment took over Gussaneh village and the Sheikh Kauwash Ridge, which admitted of a concentration of our battalion at Battalion Headquarters. We continued to hold El Kefr Hill and an important under feature of the ridge which enfiladed El Kefr Hill, and which was named the Crag picquet. This point was attacked at dawn on 6 April during a heavy mist; the attack was beaten off with a loss to us of 2 killed and 2 wounded.

In the aforementioned operations a number of very gallant deeds of bravery and endurance had been reported.

(1) In the reconnaissance on 22 March the gallant conduct of the following was brought to notice for bringing back, under heavy fire, 1 dead and 4 wounded men together with their rifles and full equipment: No. 3329 Havildar Mokkarrab Khan 58th Rifles F.F., No. 2851 Naik Tikka Khan, No. 2981 Sepoy Mian Mohommad, No. 3424 Sepoy Tikka Khan, No. 3450 Sepoy Munsibdar, No. 3382 Sepoy Sirdar Khan (all 55th Rifles, F.F.).

(2) For operations at El Kefr Hill from 27 to 29 March and subsequently Subadar Indar Singh, M.C., I.D.S.M., Subadar Kehr Singh who led their men with great dash and gallantry and

inspired all ranks with confidence and enthusiasm. Both were mentioned in despatches.

(3) No. 3413 Lance-Naik Mangal Singh of Jagraon, No. 8503 Sepoy Jainal Singh of Daska, No. 3800 Sepoy Channan Singh of Moga, No. 3099 Sepoy Channan Singh of Maler Kotla. These men showed conspicuous bravery and devotion to duty on the night of the 27/28 March at El Kefr Hill. Being constantly under heavy machine gun and artillery fire they fought the enemy machine guns with their Lewis gun silencing the enemy fire and admitting of the consolidation of the position we had gained.

(4) No. 2710 Lance-Naik Hardit Singh of Ludhiana, No. 4125 Sepoy Kelhr Singh of Kangra, No. 3337 Sepoy Sudh Singh of Gujranwala, No. 2566 Sepoy Wariam Singh of Moga. The above acted as stretcher bearers in operations at El Kefr on 27, 28 and 30 March and worked with great courage and endurance, giving first aid and bringing in wounded under very heavy fire. But for their gallantry and devotion to duty many wounded must have been left out under fire.

(5) No. 3743 Lance-Naik Hazura Singh of Moga, No. 4540 Sepoy Kesar Singh of Pasrur, No. 4620 Sepoy Shamir Singh of Amritsar, No. 4850 Sepoy Masa Singh of Moga. Above were employed as runners on 30 March during the attack on El Kefr village and were frequently sent up to get into touch with the platoons attacking the village. The enemy had counter-attacked and severed communication and the position was most obscure. The men worked their way to the front under heavy cross fire and brought back valuable information.

(6) No. 1624 Colour-Havildar Lal Khan, 55th Rifles F.F., who skilfully withdrew the remnants of the two platoons, which had attacked El Kefr village on 30 March, after all the British and Indian officers had been killed or wounded. In this operation he was most ably assisted by No. 2780 Naik Punnu Khan and No. 3450 Sepoy Munsibdar, both of the 55th Rifles F.F., who skilfully manipulated a Lewis gun on the left flank of the attack and withdrawal. These Lewis gunners expended every round they had, whereupon Sepoy Munsibdar went alone up El Kefr Hill,

where he knew an ammunition dump was located, and brought back a box of ammunition. With this Lewis gun were also No. 2851 Naik Tikka Khan and No. 2981 Sepoy Mian Mohommad, both of the 55th Rifles F.F., who covered the withdrawal of the gun from position to position and at the same time assisted several wounded men to get back under cover.

(7) Jemadar Diwana of Hamirpur (Kangra), who was left in command on El Kefr Hill when Lieutenant G. Hills advanced on El Kefr village with one platoon. He was the only Indian officer present in a very trying position where three determined counter-attacks were launched against him. The whole of his position was subjected to heavy and accurate fire, and on the steadiness of his men depended the withdrawal of the troops involved in the village fighting. Jemadar Diwana behaved throughout with conspicuous gallantry and coolness. He was awarded the Indian Order of Merit 2nd Class.

(8) No. 2841 Naik Wadhawa of Sialkot, No. 3291 Sepoy Kapura, No. 4141 Sepoy Damodar, No. 4341 Sepoy Jaimal Sing all of Hamirpur (Kangra). These four were in charge of a Lewis gun which they manipulated with great skill and effect. They held on to their position and kept up a most effective fire on the enemy, being themselves subjected to terrific fire from enemy machine guns. Their gallant action was largely responsible for the position being held. All were awarded the Indian Distinguished Service Medal.

(9) No. 3495 Sepoy Thuniya of Hamirpur (Kangra) and No. 4141 Sepoy Damodar (mentioned above) who after the fighting on 30 March had somewhat lessened, went out voluntarily and brought in a wounded man who was unable to move. They were under fire for more than 100 yards, both going and coming back.

The aforementioned are only a portion of those whose names were brought to notice for gallant conduct during actions which took place in this period of ten days and which were of a very severe nature. The circumstances under which the fighting took place were the more trying from the fact, which was obvious to all ranks, that the enemy was in strength and well organised and determined, and that our own reserves were practically nil, so that had the enemy broken through in his counter-attacks, matters would have been desperate. That so few rewards were granted for a period of fighting which was equal in severity to almost anything we had sustained in France, can only be attributed to the fact that the main objective, El Kefr village, was not captured by five platoons. This position when attacked a few days later by a full Brigade proved a very hard nut to crack.

Our casualties during the period from 22 to 31 March were 2 British, 1 Indian officer and 20 other ranks killed, 1 Indian officer and 80 other ranks wounded.

The strength of the Battalion now was 11 British and 12 Indian officers, 829 other ranks, including 160 of the 98th Infantry, attached.

Two of the British officers, Lieutenants Ekin and Abernethy who had proceeded in February to schools of instruction in scouting and signalling respectively, had been compulsorily retained as instructors at these schools; and their absence was much felt. It was thought that instructors might have been taken from so-called B class officers who were unfit for duty in the front line.

It was now considered necessary to utilise a whole Brigade supported by stokes mortars and machine guns, for the capture of the villages of El Kefr and Berukin and the intervening ridge of Sheik Nafukh. The Battalion continued to hold its position until the night of the 6/7 April when the 2nd Battalion 3rd Gurkhas (232nd Brigade) took over El Kefr Hill. During this period the hill had been constantly threatened by the enemy and bombing attacks had been of nightly occurrence.

The attack on El Kefr and Berukin bad been fixed for 9 April, and arrangements for a forward advance after these objectives had been taken were included in the orders issued. The role ordered for this Battalion was for Headquarters and half a battalion to remain in local reserve, the other half battalion would extend the road for the forward advance of guns and limbers, and escort prisoners of war. A Company and the 98th Infantry Company were detailed for the latter duty under Major A. A. Smith.

At dawn on 9 April the attack commenced. El Kefr was occupied by the 2nd Battalion 3rd Gurkhas, but they were unable to get further forward; and expected a counter-attack. On their right the village of Berukin was not captured until 15.30 hours. No further attempt to advance was made that day. On 10 April the action was renewed.

The 2nd Battalion 3rd Gurkhas, attacked a ridge, some 1,500 yards to the north, but were unable to capture it and were pinned down near the top of the ridge under enemy fire.

Headquarters, and two companies of the 58th Rifles occupied El Kefr village and A Company, from Major Smith's half battalion, was ordered to occupy El Kefr Hill in support.

B Company, under Lieutenant Gray, was sent to reinforce the 2nd Battalion 3rd Gurkhas on the advanced ridge. While crossing the open ground to the north of El Kefr village, Lieutenant Gray and 6 others were wounded and the Company went on under command of Subadar-Major Tikka Khan.

The attacks of other units on both flanks had failed and heavy casualties had been sustained. The officer commanding the 2nd Battalion 3rd Gurkhas, who had his headquarters in El Kefr village, now ordered the officers commanding the companies of his battalion on the advanced ridge to arrange for a concerted attack of all troops on the ridge, consisting of 2nd Battalion 3rd Gurkhas, a weak company of the 58th Rifles, and some 50 men of a battalion of the Hampshire Territorial Regiment. The attack was to take place at 16.45 hours, and be supported by artillery and machine gun fire.

When the moment for the attack came the advance appeared disorganised and failed to reach the top of the ridge; at the same time German troops on the ridge counter-attacked with a heavy bomb fusillade. Our own troops retired somewhat precipitously to the bottom of the ridge, but the enemy was unable to press his counter-attack owing to the strength of our machine gun fire. El Kefr village was subjected to very heavy shell fire by the enemy in which we suffered some casualties. The 2nd Battalion 3rd Gurkhas were now withdrawn, and the village and Sheikh Nafukh were held by two companies of the 58th Rifles during the ensuing night: these were relieved at dawn by the 1st Battalion 4th Welsh Regiment (53rd Division), and went into local reserve.

On the evening of 11 April the Battalion was ordered to relieve the 1st Battalion 4th Wiltshire Regiment in the line on our left. This Battalion had suffered heavy casualties during the previous day's fighting. Our Battalion took over at dusk. The position taken was neither organised nor consolidated; it was amongst huge boulders and shrubs, with a bad field of fire and view, and commanded from various points in the enemy line, making any movement by day impossible. The weather was oppressively hot and the number of unburied corpses lying out made things very unpleasant.

Our position was consolidated and held during the next five days: the enemy made no offensive movement, and on our side preparations were being made for a further advance. These preparations, however, were abandoned and orders issued to take up a strong defensive line.

This policy was largely dictated by events in France where the Germans had launched their great offensive against our line and the numerous units sent from Palestine to France during this emergency had not yet been replaced by troops from Mesopotamia and India.

During the period from 9 to 12 April, the Battalion suffered casualties, 2 British officers wounded, 7 other ranks killed, 63 wounded and 3 missing (probably killed).

Unfortunately a very large percentage of these were specialists in signalling and Lewis gunners and particularly in non-commissioned officers. Indeed, since the fighting began on 27 March the loss in non-commissioned had been very heavy and they were difficult to replace.

The work of the signallers had been magnificent. They were on continuous duty night and day, frequently out in dangerous areas to lay or mend telephone lines and keep communications efficient. Also the stretcher bearers worked most gallantly in bringing in the wounded of our own and of other units.

On the night of 12/13 April, 3704 Lance-Naik Diwan Singh of Sialkot and No. 4778 Sepoy Bhola Singh of Ludhiana showed great gallantry in rescuing and bringing in a corporal of the Wiltshire Regiment who had been lying wounded for 36 hours some 600 yards in advance of our line, and whose cries for help had been heard at intervals on 12 April after we had taken over the line from the Wiltshire Battalion. These two men had to cross the forward slopes of our own position and a nullah infested with snipers and enemy patrols. They were chased by an enemy patrol but managed to elude it and brought the wounded man back to our own line. Both were awarded the Indian Distinguished Service Medal.

On the night of 16/17 April the Battalion relieved by the 2nd Battalion 4th Hampshire Regiment, and on 18th went into camp in the Wadi Ballut as Divisional Reserve. Training and reorganisation were at once taken in hand.

On 26 April the Battalion rejoined the 234th Brigade and on 27 April took over from the 1st Battalion, 5th Duke of Cornwall's Light Infantry, a salient in the line containing the village of Rafat. This was a particularly unpleasant place, completely overlooked by the hill named Arara which was only some 750 yards from the apex of the salient. This apex, known as the ridge, was a very difficult place for troops by day as every movement was noticed and fired on; it was useless to erect shelters and the men had to lay out all day in the burning sun amongst the boulders. The salient itself was a shell trap. On 30 April the enemy made on attack on the ridge but was repulsed by artillery fire.

The Battalion held Rafat salient until 7 May when it was relieved by the 1st Battalion 4th Wiltshire Regiment, and went back to Rentis, where it remained until 26 May in Divisional Reserve.

During this period the usual disinfection and bathing was carried on, but little training could be done as large numbers of men were employed nightly as working parties on roads and defences.

The strength of the Battalion early in May was 13 British and 15 Indian officers, 820 other ranks which included 3 Indian officers and 190 other ranks of the 98th Infantry.

On 23 May, the company of the 98th Infantry left the Battalion on transfer to the 3rd Battalion 151st Infantry, a new formation. Lieutenant G. G. Hills, M.C. and Lieutenant A. C. Beynon accompanied it, a second British officer having been ordered to go with the company; Lieutenant Hills had to be detailed. His departure was much regretted by all ranks in the Battalion, in which he was very popular, and for which he had performed excellent service since joining it two and a half years previously.

On 16 May Lieutenant S. Gray, who had been wounded near El Kefr on 10 April, rejoined for duty.

At the end of May the strength of the Battalion was 10 British and 13 Indian officers, 643 other ranks.

The Battalion had now settled down to a good imitation of trench warfare, and covered a front of about 1,000 yards.

The ground was very rocky and difficult to work on as there was no depth of soil. Cover from view and passages for communication and reinforcement were quickly arranged by building up, after which the trench was deepened as far as possible and the parapet lowered and broadened.

Patrol work at night was constant and the men became very proficient in this. At the commencement of our occupation of this front the enemy was very aggressive with patrols and also with artillery, but after several patrol encounters he left no-man's-land practically free for us to move in, while our artillery rapidly assumed superiority. The month of June 1918 was passed quietly and profitably in this line, where the Battalion remained until relieved on 10 July by the 72nd Punjabis.

During this period reinforcements of 2 British officers and 80 other ranks arrived, the latter were mostly wounded and sick men returned to duty, the former were Lieutenant Green, I.A.R.O., and 2nd Lieutenant J. B. Roch (from 2nd Battalion 56th Infantry) who joined on 25 June and 3 July respectively.

Major A. A. Smith left the Battalion on 7 June to take over command of the 2nd Battalion, 151st Infantry one of the new units in course of formation.

The health of the men was satisfactory on the whole; a certain amount of stomach trouble was experienced due to the excessive number of flies.

On relief by the 72nd Punjabis the Battalion went back to the Wadi Zerka. Opportunity was afforded for a certain amount of football and sports and small parties of men were despatched to the leave camp at Ismailia which was much appreciated.

About this time it was learned that two platoons of Yusufzai were to be sent from our Depot in India as a reinforcement, and that the Government of India had every belief in their loyalty. This latter remark was doubtless for the assurance of the staff of the Division, as no such assurance was necessary to the officers of the 58th Rifles.

The Battalion remained out of the line until 30 July, during which time 4 British officers joined for duty, vizt: Lieutenant O. H. B. Dunn from the 2nd Battalion 56th Rifles F.F., Lieutenant W. J. Bradford from 1st Battalion 5th Somerset Light Infantry, and 2nd Lieutenants H. Tomlinson and E. A. Randall from the 1st Battalion 4th Duke of Cornwall Light Infantry.

Three Indian officers and 39 other ranks who left in March for furlo in India rejoined for duty on 16 July. A small furlo party of 11 other ranks and 3 followers was allowed to proceed to India on 24 July.

On 30 July the Battalion, strength 17 British and 14 Indian officers, 774 other ranks, took over the Rafat sector, including the village of that name, from the 3rd Battalion 3rd Gurkhas.

At this time the Battalion was organised as under:
A Company two platoons Dogras and two platoons Sikhs,
B Company all Punjabi Mohommadans,
C Company all Sikhs,
D Company two platoons Punjabi Mohommadans, the remaining two platoons of D Company were to be composed of Yusufzai on their arrival which, as previously mentioned, was expected about the end of August.

The defences of Rafat had been reorganised by R. E. assisted by large working parties. Trenches and sangars had been made and the perimeter considerably shortened by vacating the ridge, which had been such an unpleasant spot to hold when the Battalion occupied it early in May. The place was, however, a shell trap, as the 3rd Battalion 3rd Gurkhas found to their cost, when Rafat was heavily shelled a few days before we took over from them.

Refugee inhabitants from the enemy side of the line came almost daily to our lines and were sent back to Divisional Headquarters. They reported great scarcity of food and water. They confirmed the reports of our observers, that the strongpoint of Arara, just north of Rafat and positions to the east of it were held by German troops.

Some good work was done by night patrols, but the country was covered with dry, crisp, undergrowth, through which it was impossible to move quietly. A strong patrol of 25 men under Captain Ekin, and Subadar Indar Singh M.C., I.D.S.M., had a tough fight on the night of 10/11 August. Having arrived within fifty yards of an enemy picquet, they were about to rush it, when flankers reported enemy parties moving round both flanks to cut them off. As the same moment they were heavily fired on from front and flanks. The patrol, slowly moving back, succeeded in holding up both flank attacks, and reached our wire with a loss of 4 wounded, who were all brought in. A few days later a patrol of the 123rd Riles from our left, found 3 dead enemy on the ground where the encounter took place.

The Battalion remained at Rafat until the night 11/12 August, when it was relieved by the 123rd (Outram's) Rifles and moved back to Rentis. During this period Lieutenant J. E. D. Manlove from 110th Jats reported his arrival for duty, and Lieutenant Tomlinson 1st Battalion 4th Duke of Cornwall Light Infantry (attached) departed to join the 39th Royal Fusiliers, a new formation composed of British subject Jews, to which race Lieutenant Tomlinson belonged. On 15 August Lieutenant-Colonel A. G. Lind, D.S.O., was granted three weeks leave on urgent private affairs to the United Kingdom, and handed over temporary command of the Battalion to Major R. de W. Waller.

The Battalion remained at Rentis until 23 August, when it relieved the 1st Battalion 4th Duke of Cornwall's Light Infantry in the line to the north of Deir Ballut.

While at Rentis, in part compliance with a scheme to bring the strength of British officers in Indian Army units up to 30, together with a staff of British non-commissioned officers, instructors, and assistants, the following officers and British other ranks joined the Battalion: Lieutenants J. Bulleid, A. H. C. Allen, and D. W. Locke with 16 sergeants, all of the 2nd Battalion 4th Devon Regiment.

All these had to be instructed so as to get a working knowledge of Hindustani before they could be of much use. The non-commissioned officers were distributed amongst companies for instructing (as far as possible) in Lewis gun and bombing: others being employed by the Quartermaster and the Transport Officer. Looking back on the results of this experiment it is doubtful if it was of much use. The non-commissioned officers were territorials and not professional soldiers and were no better, and in some cases not so well, instructed as our own Indian non-commissioned officers. They did however pull their weight in the transport and quartermaster's departments for which they had more special knowledge and aptitude. They had no knowledge of the Indian soldier and, except in a few cases, were unlikely to earn his respect. It was a different matter to that which obtained of sending British non-commissioned officers to the Egyptian Army, these were amongst the best of our professional soldiers, and were first class instructors. Nor could it compare with the same custom which obtained with the Indian Army in pre-mutiny days when the non-commissioned officers attached to battalions had had considerable experience of Indians and spoke their language fluently.

From the portion of the line in which the Battalion was now located, the nearest enemy position was 800 yards distant. A patrol discovered an old enemy battery position, between the lines, which contained some 200 shells and shell cases, these were brought in two days later by a working party covered by a patrol.

The Battalion remained in this sector of the line until the night of 30/31 August, when it was relieved by two companies of a French battalion of *Tirailleurs*, known as the *Detachment Francais de Palestine et Syrie*. To make up for their weakness in bayonet strength they had no less than thirty-six machine guns, and when handing over the line, whenever a weak spot was pointed out to the French Commander his invariable reply was *Ah! Bon: Mitrailleuse, Mitrailleuse*. This French detachment had recently joined the forces under General Allenby, and two of its officers had spent two days with our Battalion early in August. These said that their force consisted chiefly of Armenians who had fled from Russia to America, in which country they had been recruited.

The Battalion marched back to Beit Nabala in the early hours of 1 September. Here it was to undergo special training with the other battalions of the Brigade. It had a strength at this time of 15 British and 11 Indian officers, 37 British other ranks and 678 Indian other ranks.

On 11 September Lieutenant Potbury joined the Battalion for duty on transfer from the 2nd Battalion 4th Devon Regiment.

Although no official information had been given it was now obvious that a 'push' on a large scale was about to take place. Trenches were mapped out, with lines and flags, in exact imitation of the enemy trenches which would be assaulted, and which had been photographed from the air. The Brigade was deployed upon the same front and in the order of battle it would employ on the day of the attack.

This training continued until 16 September on which day the Battalion marched after dark to Mulebbis.

On this day also a reinforcement, consisting of 113 (two strong platoons) Yusufzais, 65 Punjabi Mohommadans, 44 Sikhs and 14 Dogras, arrived under command of Subadar Ajun Khan, I.D.S.M.

Most of the Yusufzai were recruits, with a stiffening of some of the old non-commissioned officers and a few men from amongst those who had formerly been with the Battalion.

It was a great pity that such a large and partly trained reinforcement, which had arrived from India some weeks before and been retained at the Kantara Base Depot, should not have been sent sooner to join its battalion, and have had the benefit of the previous two weeks training, instead of being sent to arrive just on the eve of an important action. However, the reinforcement was a good one, men of our own unit and trained at our own depot, and the Battalion was right glad to greet them. At this time a slight epidemic of influenza was spreading and had caused a number of casualties in all units. This epidemic later became worldwide and caused vast and widespread loss of life, especially in the Punjab where almost a million people perished.

The day of 17 September 1918 was spent in the orange groves west of Mulebbis: the strictest secrecy was being observed and comprehensive orders issued for the prevention of the least movement by day. Indeed, the whole preparation for this last great action in Palestine had been carried out with the utmost secrecy. The plan was cleverly conceived and the preliminary movements of troops and their final concentration at the place of assembly were masterpieces of staff work. Camouflage was carried to such a degree that less than forty-eight hours before the action commenced it was reported in the Egyptian papers, probably with truth, that the Commander-in-Chief, General Allenby, had been sea bathing near Alexandria.

On the night of the 17/18 September the Battalion marched to its position of assembly behind a point in the line known as the Cockshy. Preliminary orders were received for an attack on the Turkish position on a fifteen miles front from Rafat to the sea. Later it was made known that the assault would commence at 4.30 a.m. on the morrow, 19 September.

The general orders for the 234th Brigade were that it would capture the strongly held Tabsor position, the 232nd Brigade being on its right and the 7th Indian (Meerut) Division on its left. At the commencement of the attack, the Brigade would cover a front of 1,000 yards with two Battalions, these being the 1st Battalion 152nd Indian Infantry on the right and the 58th Rifles F.F. on the left. Two companies of the Somerset Light Infantry were to capture an important work F-13, known as Machine Gun Hill, just in front of the enemy trench system and between the two battalions mentioned above. They covered a front of 200 yards. Our battalion was to advance on a front of 400 yards, capture the village of Tabsor and the defence system for 500 yards to the east of the village – gradually spreading out until, when it reached its initial objective 8,000 yards distant, it would be covering a front of about 1,000 yards. By 4.20 a.m. on 19 September the Battalion was in position on the enemy side of our wire, where lines had been taped out for the first and second waves, these being 150 yards distant from each other. The first wave consisted of A Company (Captain Ekin) on the left, and B Company (Lieutenant Bradford) on the right, the second wave C Company (Captain Gillespie) on the left and D Company (Lieutenant Dunn) on the right. Headquarters, with four Lewis gun detachments in reserve, moved immediately in rear of the second wave.

Map VII shows the lines of advance of our battalion, the forming up line is marked A-B, also the right and left boundaries are marked. The final objective was some 1,500 yards beyond the trench system marked C-D where the Battalion finally halted, as is detailed further on, to allow of the turning manoeuvre of the 7th (Meerut) Division.

At 4.30 a.m. an intense bombardment was opened by all our guns and machine guns, and the assault moved forward under the barrage. Within three minutes the enemy counter-barrage commenced. It fell most heavily on our second wave and Battalion Headquarters which, however, moving steadily forward, were soon clear of it.

At 4.47 a.m. the enemy's front line was penetrated and those of the garrison who had not fled surrendered. A few strong points with machine guns resisted, but were quickly overpowered and the garrisons bayoneted. Tabsor village was encircled and the garrison fled in a westerly direction, mostly falling into the hands of the 92nd Punjabis on our left.

During the advance to this first objective, the Battalion was on a much broader front than was intended. The greater part of a battalion of the 232nd Brigade on our right mysteriously retired when the enemy counter-barrage fell amongst them. In order to fill the gap thus created, the 1st Battalion 152nd Indian Infantry closed towards their right. B Company, realising the situation also extended their front towards the right and A Company similarly conformed. Tabsor village, therefore, for the assault on which the whole of A Company had been specially detailed, actually encircled and taken by a mere handful (about twenty men) under Captain Ekin, and Jemadar Thakur Sing.

At 5.26 a.m., the enemy second line was reached where a ten minutes halt, according to programme, allowed of reorganisation and adjustment of line and direction. But the dust and smoke caused by our own barrage and the smoke screen used by the enemy made it impossible to see more than fifty yards ahead, no points were recognisable and direction had to be maintained by compass. Except for dead and the wounded, the enemy's second line was empty.

The Battalion again moved forward and pushed along without incident: being somewhat ahead of scheduled time it was stopped to conform with the movement of the 1st Battalion, 152nd Infantry, which had been checked for a while. Touch was thus lost with the 92nd Punjabis on our left, as that battalion pressed on.

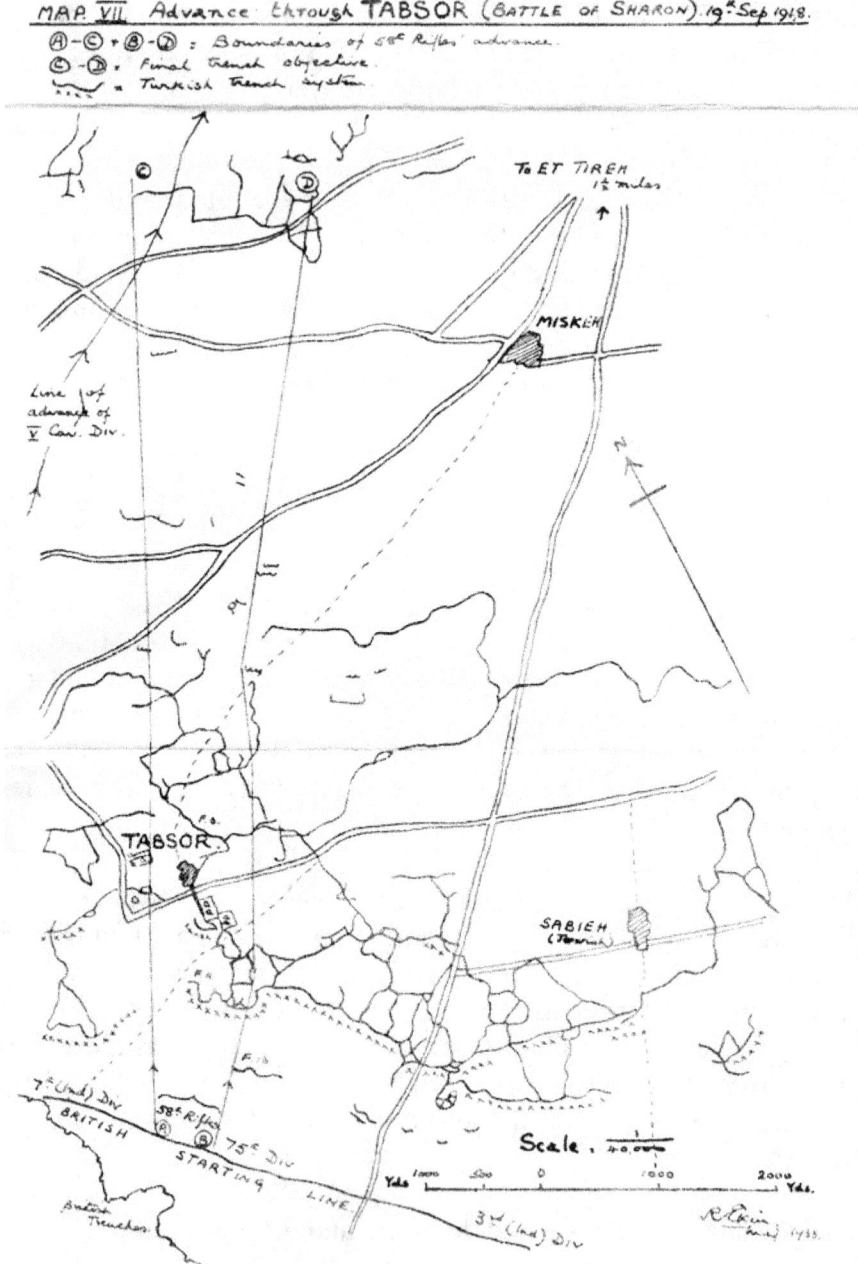

Moving forward to a low ridge to its front our Battalion was shelled by 6-inch howitzers of our own artillery, and although red flares were lit (according to general orders) and our own aeroplanes flying just above were signalled, the shelling continued and casualties were suffered. The Battalion, therefore, moved forward again, the Lewis guns coming into action against the retreating enemy. The final objective was reached at 8 a.m. and at the same time the 1st Guides Infantry F.F. of the 7th Indian Division arrived on the same spot, claiming the system of trenches as their own objective and the point of pivot for the turning movement of the 7th Indian Division, eastwards across the front of the 75th Division.

The Battalion was, therefore, closed to its right to allow for this manoeuvre of the 7th Division. So far as our Battalion was concerned, its operations in this, the last and most successful action of the Palestine campaign, had now come to an end.

The 75th Division here came into Corps Reserve, and our only further connection with the enemy consisted in helping to guard and escort the thousands of prisoners sent back by our cavalry and the more fortunate divisions of our infantry, which pushed on ceaselessly until the enemy had been cleared out of Palestine and Syria.

In this action our Battalion was opposed by the 61st Regiment of the 20th Turkish Division –reported to be a 'crack' corps. We captured about one hundred prisoners, six machine guns, two 77-millimetre guns and a 5.9-inch howitzer besides many animals and much material.

Our casualties, which were caused chiefly by the enemy counter-barrage, were Lieutenant Alan, (2nd Battalion the Devon Regiment, attached) and Subadar Mohammad Arabi I.O.M., wounded: 7 Indian other ranks killed and 2 British and 37 Indian other ranks wounded.

The day was hot and the dust and smoke terrific, and the men suffered severely from thirst, as all connection with enemy watering places was strictly prohibited and our own water did not arrive until dusk.

Contrary to expectation our task had not been a difficult one; the Tabsor defences were formidable, deep and well-sited trenches behind wire and heavy cactus hedges, but the surprise and suddenness of the attack, combined with a terrific bombardment had completely unnerved the enemy on our front and he offered only slight and isolated resistance.

Amongst those brought to notice for gallantry and devotion to duty in this action were: Lieutenant A. H. C. Allen, 2nd Battalion, 4th Devon Regiment (attached) who was commanding the party told off to follow up the second wave of the Battalion and dispose of any enemy remaining in strong points or dug-outs after our attack had passed over them: commonly known as "mopper-up". This work he carried through most effectively. Although shot through the shoulder before he reached the first objective, he continued to lead his men and direct operations until the last objective, some three miles forward, had been disposed of. He was awarded the Military Cross.

Nos 2938 Lance-Naik Prithann Sing of Jammu and 651 Sepoy Fairu of Jammu of A Company, with four others of their section who were killed in the encounter, rounded up an enemy strongpoint held by twenty-five enemy with two machine guns. They put the machine guns out of action, bayoneted four of the enemy, and kept the remainder engaged until assistance came, when all the enemy and guns were captured. Both were awarded the Indian Distinguished Service Medal.

No. 4263 Sepoy Bar Singh of Jhind, No. 4387 Sepoy Amar Singh of Ferozepur, and No. 4707 Sepov Hakam Singh of Sialkot, who were on the left flank of our line, observed an enemy strongpoint garrisoned by a detachment and two machine guns harassing our left front and the unit on our left. These three promptly attacked the point, got through the wire, killed four enemy and captured an officer and one other. All were awarded the Indian Distinguished Service Medal.

Captain R. G. Ekin, Captain D. S. Gillespie, Lieutenant O. H. Dunn, and Lieutenant W. J. Bradford, were all brought to notice for gallant and skilful leading of their companies. It was due to the personal control and good leadership of these officers, ably assisted by their platoon commanders, that the advance was so successful. All were mentioned in despatches.

Subadar Kehr Singh of Moga was suffering from a high fever on the night before the attack, but refused to report sick: and throughout the day led his men with great gallantry and captured a strongpoint with a machine gun and 15 enemy, the men he led being mostly recruits who had joined two days before. He was mentioned in despatches.

Major R. de W. Waller who commanded the Battalion most ably in this great success was awarded the Distinguished Service Order.

Until 29 September the Battalion remained in and about the Kalkiliyeh district carrying out salvage work, which was interspersed with spasmodic attempts at training exercises, ordered by the Divisional staff. The dullness of this work, aggravated as it was by daily reports of fresh victories in France, Italy and Bulgaria and the rapid and successful advance of our own troops ahead in Syria, had a most depressing effect on the rank and file, and the so-called 'Spanish influenza' epidemic, which was now causing considerable apprehension, began seriously to affect the men. As many as ninety were attending sick parade daily of who some forty were evacuated to Field Ambulances. The sick report for 20 and 21 September showed 2 British and 2 Indian officers and 76 other ranks admitted to hospital.

On 29 September the Battalion was sent for a short rest to the sea shore, where bathing could be indulged in and from which it derived much benefit.

During this period Lieutenant F. H. Simons (27th Cavalry) reported his arrival for duty with the Battalion.

On 3 October the Battalion marched to the neighbourhood of El Tireh where the ground, lately occupied by Turkish troops, was extremely foul and the swarms of flies incredible.

On 17 October Lieutenant-Colonel Lind, D.S.O. rejoined the Battalion from leave in the United Kingdom and resumed command.

During October the Battalion moved from El Tireh to Yenna and thence to Kerkur where charge was taken of the prisoners of war camp. Thousands of prisoners were being passed through, for whose custody and safe escort as far as Tul Keram our guards were responsible.

The bivouac camp at Kerkur was covered with long coarse grass and scrub, infested by scorpions, chiefly small ones but capable of inflicting a painful sting.

On 18 October, Lieutenant C. S. McLaren and 74 rank and file of the 57th Rifles F.F. reported for duty with this unit and on 25 October, Lieutenant A. H. C Allen, M.C., with 2 Indian officers and 111 other ranks rejoined from hospital.

On 31 October the welcome news was received of the conclusion with the Turkish nation of an Armistice, the terms of which amounted to an unconditional surrender.

The certainty of the approaching success of our armies in Europe was reflected in the spontaneously joyous behaviour of all ranks on the evening of the announcement of the Turkish surrender.

There was no longer any need for the 75th Division to be retained in Palestine – preparations were made to entrain for a move and we knew, not without some slight regret, that we must look forward to long days and weeks in camps near our base, until arrangements could be made for our return to India.

About this period a number of British officers were posted to the Battalion from time to time for duty. It was learned that in anticipation of heavy casualties occurring amongst British officers in the fighting on 19 September, a large number of officers had been sent to Palestine from England, Salonika and Egypt. Practically all were of the British service; they knew no Hindustani and most had no wish to join the Indian Army. The notification of their arrival stated that they were 'temporarily attached and liable to be removed at short notice.'

During October and November the following officers joined the Battalion: Lieutenant C. A. Woodruffe, Captain A. B. F. T. Stevenson (4th Royal Irish Rifles), 2nd Lieuts L. E. Watts, K. N. Woodhouse, G. A. Stannard (3rd Norfolk Regiment), Major C. L. Oliver (4th Middlesex Regiment), 2nd Lieutenant E. F. Stacey (5th Middlesex Regiment), and 2nd Lieutenant J. Bullied (2nd Battalion 4th Devon Regiment).

As, within the next two month, all these officers left the Battalion to be demobilised or absorbed in their own units, they will not be referred to again. On 2 November, 2nd Lieutenant W. P. Fogarty, 57th Rifles F.F. reported his arrival for duty with the Battalion.

On 8 November the Battalion marched from Kerkur to rejoin the 234th Brigade and accompanied the Brigade to the concentration camp at Haditheh.

On 4 November news of the capitulation of Austria was received; followed on 11 November by the announcement of the Armistice with Germany. One heard the news of the end of the Great War with a feeling of great gladness mingled with regret. Gladness and Pride at having defeated the greatest military power the world had known and regret that those who had died gloriously in the achievement were not bodily present to share our gladness, and, though not with us, will ever live in our memories.

The Battalion was to move yet once again before its departure from Palestine and on 18 November, took over from the Kashmir Imperial Service Infantry, a former German Colony known as Sarona, two and a half miles from Jaffa. Here the Battalion remained contentedly in camp until 3 December, when, having handed over Sarona to an Italian unit, it marched to Ludd, preparatory to entraining for the Infantry Base at Kantara. Its strength was 22 British officers (including 10 attached) 14 Indian officers, 33 British and 596 Indian other ranks.

On 5 December the Battalion entrained quietly and efficiently in two trains and arrived at Kantara at midnight. Some delay occurred in reaching camp as, on arrival of the second train, it was learned that the last few trucks, containing most of the transport animals, had become detached some three miles from Kantara, owing to the break of a coupling, and the rest of the train had gone on, the engine driver having noticed no difference. Camp was found, located at the 5th kilo stone on the road from Kantara to El Arish, and here the Battalion was destined to remain for over two months.

The question of education was now taken up seriously. Large numbers of men volunteered for school, and company schools were started.

Large working parties were demanded daily for clearing huge dumps of stores, clothing and ammunition. Kantara presented the appearance of a great canvas city: it was estimated that over 50,000 men were camped there.

During December, 2 Indian officers and 110 other ranks of the 57th Rifles F.F., joined the Battalion, and 303 other ranks of our Battalion rejoined from hospital, detachments, courses of instruction and various extra regimental employment.

The strength of the Battalion on 31 December 1918 was 20 British and 15 Indian officers, 29 British and 1,008 Indian other ranks with 33 transport drivers attached, and 48 followers.

CHAPTER VI
Egypt, 1919

The Battalion remained in camp at Kantara East until 17 March 1919, when it proceeded to Suez to embark for India. During this period as much military and educational training and recreation was carried on as circumstances allowed. Up to 4 February half the Battalion worked daily at clearing the ordnance dumps. Thereafter duties consisted chiefly in sharing guards with the 123rd Outram's Rifles over the Turk prisoners of war and escorting train loads of rations to Ludd.

No information was given as to the probable date of return to India, but it appeared from the sequence in which Battalions left Kantara for Suez that the new formations would be the first to go, the old battalions probably last, this being a matter of economy and expediency

On 9 February Subadars Ajun Khan I.D.S.M. and Madat Khan with 26 other ranks and 2 followers proceeded with a large party, for which arrangements had been made to visit Mecca. Very few men volunteered to accompany this party, the reason being understood to be that as this was not the time of year laid down for the pilgrimage this would not count as *pukka hajj*.

During January four of our men taken prisoner by the Germans and now on their way to India, visited the Battalion. They stated that they, in company with most Indian prisoners of war had been sent to do agricultural work in Rumania when that country was overrun by the Germans. On the whole they appear to have been well treated, but were largely dependent on, and most grateful for, the parcels of food and clothing sent them from time to time by the committee of the Indian prisoners of war fund: and these parcels seem to have been delivered fairly regularly.

In the sports and games held during this period the Battalion did well, taking nearly all the prizes in the Brigade sports and many in the Divisional sports. The latter include first prizes in wrestling, relay race, cross country race, putting the weight and hundred yards race, second prizes in the half mile, one mile and Indian officers' race. At the end of February chosen representatives from all the divisions and formations of the Egyptian Expeditionary Force met at Cairo to compete. In these, the Battalion took gold medals for winning the relay and half mile races and bronze medal for third place in the hundred yards. In the Divisional hockey the Battalion was beaten in the final contest by a very fine team of Queen Victoria's Own Sappers and Miners.

On 4 February, according to instructions, an advance party of 2 Indian officers and 28 other ranks, under command of Captain G. R. Dowland, M.C., proceeded to India to join the Depot.

On the 27 February all ranks of the 59th Rifles F.F. attached, were sent to rejoin their own unit in Palestine.

During January and February all the British other ranks attached to this Battalion were either demobilised or returned to British units.

On 15 March, orders were received to entrain for Suez and on 17 March the following strength entrained at Kantara: 8 British and 12 Indian officers, 1 Assistant Surgeon, 977 other ranks, 25 drivers and 31 followers.

The Divisional and Brigade Commanders and staff saw the Battalion off.

This severed the connection of the Battalion with the 75th Division, Egyptian Expeditionary Force in which formation it had served since the 14 September 1917.

On the 19 March rumours were current in Suez that a massacre of Europeans had taken place in Southern Egypt and that a rebellion of Egyptians was breaking out in various parts of the country.

Demonstrations were expected in Suez and orders were received to send guards to protect the railway station, the oil refinery, docks and important public buildings and factories in Suez, and Port Tewfiq. No demonstrations, however, took place. The Egyptians at Suez are somewhat isolated from the rest of the country, and they are not a stout-hearted race and did not like our looks; under the circumstances they doubtless considered discretion the better part of valour. The risings in Egypt were widespread however. Early in April it was rumoured that the Egyptian Army and Police were untrustworthy and that no more troops could leave the country until it had been quietened.

On 14 April orders were received for the Battalion to move to Cairo. It entrained on 15th and arrived at Cairo the same day, and marched to the Polygon camp at Abbasia, where it was located in wooden huts. The Battalion remained here until 5 May in readiness to suppress disturbances in Cairo, but none took place.

During April the following awards were notified in the *Gazette of India*, No. 461 of 1919: Subadar-Major Tikka Khan to the 2nd Class of the Order of British India, for gallantry and devotion to duty while serving in the field with the Egyptian Expeditionary Force. No. 536 of 1919: Major A. A. Smith, Captain R. G. Ekin, Subadar Indar Singh, M.C., I.D.S.M., No. 3503 Havildar Jainal Singh and 3413 Havildar Mangal Singh were mentioned in Despatches for gallantry and devotion to duty for the period covering 18 March 1918 to 18 September 1918.

On 5 May the Battalion was ordered to Minia, a large town in Upper Egypt, and to take over, also, garrison duties at Beni Mazar, a small town some thirty miles north of Minia. Headquarters with B and D Companies left Cairo in the early morning and arrived at Minia the same evening, being met by Brigadier-General E. M. Colston C.M.G., D.S.O., M.V.O., commanding 'Colstons Force' under whom, when he was commanding the 233rd Brigade, the Battalion had served in Palestine in March and April 1918.

The Battalion was located in two cotton factories, and took over duties from the 1st Battalion 5th Somerset Light Infantry and detachments of the 29th Punjabis. A and C Companies under Captain D. S. Gillespie left Cairo on 7 May and the same day took over duties at Beni Mazar from a half battalion of Somerset Light Infantry.

Another detachment of two platoons under Lieutenant W. P. Fogarty was sent from Minia to Kerkas, twelve miles south of Minia, to guard a sugar factory of some commercial importance. The Battalion was now incorporated in the 10th Division as part of the army of occupation in Egypt. Minia was a town which had distinguished itself by attempting to form a Government of its own – a local Soviet in fact headed by a doctor, and a Sheikh who were the real instigators in the rising. The trial by Court-Martial of the six ring leaders took place in May and June in Minia. Two were sentenced to death: the remainder to long terms of imprisonment.

The population of the town, however, were quite friendly and respectful. The Battalion occasionally marched through the streets and bazaars, and the bugle band performed twice a week in one of the main thoroughfares. No trouble was experienced from the local population during the five months the Battalion was located at Minia and Beni Mazar.

During May, Captain S. T. Gray and Lieutenant H. C. B. Lyon were demobilised while on leave in England. Captain Gray joined the Battalion in May 1915, and served with it continuously thereafter. He was a New Zealander, had been to Oxford University, and when the war broke out was employed with Mr Tyndale-Biscoe's medical mission in Kashmir. He immediately joined the Indian Army Reserve of officers and after six months training in India was sent to France.

At the end of May 1919 furlo to India was re-opened for men having urgent cases.

On 1 June the Battalion came officially under the administration of the 29th Brigade, 10th Division, commanded by Brigadier-General C. R. Smith, V.C., M.C.

Brigadier-General E. M. Colston, C.M.G., D.S.O., M.V.O, left Minia on relief and the Minia Mudiriyat came under the military jurisdiction of the officer commanding 58th Rifles F.F.

The Battalion was now practically certain to remain in Egypt for an indefinite period. Training was a matter of considerable difficulty in a place like Minia where the whole surrounding county was under cultivation. However, use was made of a large tract of ground which had been commandeered by Government as an aeroplane landing ground and in one corner of this a short range was made and some very necessary musketry carried out.

Considerable disappointment was doubtless felt (but not expressed) amongst the rank and file at the retention of the Battalion in Egypt. Many men had written home in March to say that they would arrive in India in April. Marriages had been arranged and serious financial loss was anticipated through being unable to carry out marriage contracts. The influenza epidemic which had ravished the Punjab in the early spring had left many homes unprotected. Moreover, no letters were now being received from India. This, perhaps, was as well as they would have told of the riots in the Punjab and increased the feeling of unrest. Furlo had been sanctioned for ten percent provided reinforcements were available from India, but owing to the Afghan attacks on frontier posts the Indian Government were unable to send any reinforcements; so only a few very urgent cases could be allowed to leave the Battalion.

On 16 June the troops were withdrawn from the cotton factories, which were now commencing to resume work, and went into a camp just to the north of the town.

On 19 June Lieutenant-General Sir E. S. Bulfin, K.C.B., commanding troops in Egypt, accompanied by Brigadier-General Peerles, visited Mina and expressed his satisfaction at all he saw.

During this month the following officers joined the Battalion for duty: Captain E. M. Ashton, Lieutenant M. B. P. Reeve and Lieutenant T. L. Evans.

The Treaty of Versailles was signed by the Germans on 28 June, and 30 June was proclaimed a public holiday. A reception was held at Battalion Headquarters by the officer commanding as representative of the King-Emperor at which the Mudir, the foreign consuls, the officials and notables of Minia and the District, and the leading clergy of various denominations in Minia were present: some eighty in all; congratulations on victory and peace were exchanged.

The 14 July was proclaimed as a general holiday throughout Egypt for peace celebrations. A luncheon party was given by the Mudir of Minia to which all the officers were invited together with all British officials in the Mudiriyat of Minia together with many Egyptian and Bedouin notables. In the afternoon a ceremonial parade was held on the aeroplane landing ground at which the Mudir and all officials in the Mudiriyat were present. The salute was taken by Lieutenant-Colonel A. G. Lind, D.S.O., commanding troops in the Mudiriyat. This was followed by sports in which men of the Battalion competed very favourably with Egyptian and Bedouin police. Riding displays by Bedouins chiefs and their followers were given. An enormous crowd of Egyptians gathered on the ground and the general tone of the meeting was most friendly.

In July orders were received to select and send three representatives of the Battalion to accompany the Indian contingent that was to take part in the peace celebrations held in London in August 1919. The following were selected: Acting Subadar-Major Indar Singh, M.C., No. 3336 acting Havildar-Major Mir Mohommad (P.M.) and No. 3921 Lance-Naik Kapura (Dogra), Langri Ugarsain accompanied them. These returned the following October. Subadar Indar Singh received his Military Cross decoration from the hands of His Majesty The King-Emperor. This party was greatly impressed by what they saw in England. They extolled the English milk and meat with which they seem to have been liberally supplied, as each man had put on considerable weight since his departure three months before. Underground London, the Boy Scouts and the cattle in the Royal Park at Windsor appear to have made the greatest impression on their minds.

On 25 July sports were held by the 10th Division at Cairo. Representatives from the Battalion obtained first prizes in the 100 yards, 220 yards, quarter-mile, half-mile, three miles races and the relay race; second places in the quarter, one mile and three miles races; and third places in the long jump, high jump and half mile race: being easily first in the Division.

On 4 August the bodies of eight British officers and other ranks who had been murdered and mutilated by an Egyptian mob in the train at Deirut station on 18 March 1919, and removed later on from the train at Minia by the Greek community there and buried by them in their own cemetery, were exhumed by men of the Battalion under directions of a British burial party and the bodies placed in coffins. A detachment of 5 officers and 300 rank and file of the 22nd Battalion the Manchester Regiment arrived at Minia the same day. In the evening the coffins were placed on the Battalion limbers and taken with full military honours to the railway station, about one mile distant, and placed in a special train. The route to the station was lined by the Battalion and the Manchesters. About one hundred mourners followed the coffins including the Mudir of Minia and all Egyptian Government officials, all British officers, the British and Greek communities of Minia and a number of Coptic notables. The procession was watched by a very large and silent crowd of local inhabitants. The special train left for Cairo next morning escorted by the Manchesters' detachment and preceded by an armoured train. A guard of honour of the Battalion saluted the train as it left the platform.

On 8 August the Battalion was inspected by Major-General Sir G. F. Gorringe, K.C.B., C.M.G., D.S.O., commanding the 10th Division who expressed himself as highly satisfied. He was especially pleased with the mounted infantry. This consisted of ten men from each company who, under Jemadar Misri Khan, who was formerly in a cavalry regiment, were mounted on the Battalion transport mules and at this time were becoming a very efficient body of men. The mules were fine American animals, few being under fourteen hands, and were kept in splendid condition.

On 14 August a party of 107 of all ranks left the Battalion for India; of these 76 were for eight weeks urgent leave, in India, the remainder for Depot duty or discharge.

On the 15th August a second party of 22 under Subadar Mohommad Arabi Khan, I.O.M., proceeded to Suez en route to Mecca for the pilgrimage.

During the month the whole detachment at Beni Mazar was withdrawn to Minia, its place being taken by Egyptian police.

The following awards appeared in the *Gazette of India* for July 1919: Mentioned in Despatches, Major R. de W. Waller, D.S.O., and Captain D. B. Mackenzie. Major Waller was at this time on sick leave in England, and Captain Mackenzie had left the Battalion on 19 May to take up an appointment under the Palestine Occupied Enemy Territory Administration.

On 19 September the Battalion was inspected by Lieutenant-General Sir W. N. Congreve, V.C., K.C.B., Commanding-in-Chief in Egypt, whose father and son had also earned that coveted decoration the Victoria Cross.

He was accompanied by his chief of the staff Major-General Sir L. J. Bols, K.C.B., and Major-General Sir G.F. Gorringe, K.C.B., commanding the 10th Division. The inspection was most satisfactory.

On 25 September one company of the 72nd Punjabis arrived at Minia and took over the duties, and our Battalion left the same evening for Damanhour.

The whole Minia area had been very quiet since the arrival there of the Battalion five months previous, and though there were occasional rumours of intended risings and other alarms, nothing ever materialised; and the area was to all appearances in a contented frame of mind, to which an excellent cotton crop doubtless contributed.

Lieutenant F. H. Simons, (probationer for the Indian Army) joined the Battalion on 20 September for duty.

At this time letters from India for the men, which since April had come very irregularly, owing to men having written in March to announce their early return to India, were now coming in frequently and regularly. These letters did not as a rule bring good news. They spoke of the non-fulfilment of marriage contracts, threatening financial loss; of the deaths of parents and relations from disease, chiefly due to the influenza epidemic which had ravished the Punjab, and urging early discharge or leave to look after land and property; the latter was frequently spoken of as being unattended, or exploited by people who had no right to it. As no reinforcements could be sent from India owing to the war with Afghanistan and trouble in Waziristan, it was impossible to allow more than a few very urgent cases to proceed to India.

On 10 October the Battalion was inspected by Brigadier-General W. A. Blake, C.M.G., D.S.O., commanding the 29th Brigade to which the Battalion was now attached.

On 12 October Lieutenant W. P. Fogerty, 57th Rifles F.F. (attached) met with a fatal accident. He had been out hunting and was retuning on a goods train. Just before the train started, one of the hounds jumped out of an open truck in which it had been placed. Lieutenant Fogerty got down, caught the hound and was lifting it into the truck when the train started. Lieutenant Fogerty fell with one leg under the train and a wheel passed over it and crushed the bone. The medical officer in the hospital at Ras-el-Tin (Alexandria) tried to save the leg and did not decide to amputate it until 19 October. Unfortunately gangrene had set in and Lieutenant Fogerty died in hospital on 20 October. He was buried in the military cemetery at Hadra (Alexandria) with full military honours. The Sherwood Foresters provided the firing party.

Damanhour is a fairly large town with a college for students, and being situated between Alexandria and Tanta, both troublesome and seditious towns, was somewhat adversely affected towards the British. During October 1919 there was much excitement in Egypt in connection with the Milner Commission sent out from England to endeavour to decide on a *modus vivendi* between the British Government in Egypt and the claim of the Egyptians to complete independence. There were several attempts at 'demonstrations' in Damanhour but they never materialised into anything serious. The Battalion marched through the town a few times and the mounted infantry were frequently sent through the streets 'for exercise', all of which had a calming effect on the minds of the would-be demonstrators. One of the most important places in the Damanhour area was El Aft, twelve miles distant, where was located the pumping station which pumped water from the Nile river into the Mahmudieh Canal on which the water supply of Alexandria was dependent. This station was never actually threatened, but a careful watch on it was kept.

On 23 October a mobile column, consisting of two companies, under Captain C. R. Spear, was sent on a three days' march in order that troops might be seen by inhabitants of the district. The column returned on 25th having covered forty-five miles. These mobile columns continued to be sent frequently and the effect was decidedly good both on the physical health of the men and the moral health of the populace.

On 30 October a company was sent to Sidi Bisher near Alexandria to relieve the 46th Punjabis of the duty of guarding Turkish prisoners of war. They were required to deal with trouble which appeared to be brewing in Alexandria. These troubles materialised about the 17 November and for several days there were riots, and the military had to be called on to assist the civil police. The Egyptian ministry resigned and there were strong rumours of attacks by Bedouin on camps and Europeans. The local Mudir was warned that if demonstrations or riots took place in Dananhour, vigorous action would be taken. He consequently ordered the closing of all schools and the students' college: and the students were sent away to their homes thus removing the most likely cause of trouble.

On 25 November a party of 2 Indian officers and 60 other ranks proceeded to India on furlo, these being men most of whom had served continuously overseas without leave for three years and a few men with very urgent reasons for leave.

Gazette of India Notification No. 3159 of 1919 announced the promotion to the rank of Brevet Lieutenant-Colonel of Major J. D. M. Flood, 58th Rifles F.F. for distinguished work in India during the war, and subsequent operations on the North-West Frontier.

On 5 December a small company of the 1st Battalion the Guides, consisting of 2 British and 3 Indian officers and 102 other ranks, joined the Battalion for duty, in replacement of C Company (Sikhs) which had been sent to Sidi Bisher prisoner of war camp.

On 12 December thirty mounted infantry were sent on a three days march through the district. They covered thirty miles the first day. On the second day they were met by the Commanding Officer who had come out with a few men in light Ford cars, and surrounded and searched for arms the village of Kom Zimran. On the third day the mounted infantry returned having covered eighty-five miles in the three days. The mules were in very good condition – no sore backs. The demeanour of the inhabitants was reported as being more surly than before.

An assault at arms was held after Christmas which included riding, bicycling, driving, shooting and tent pegging events. Most of the British, the local inhabitants, the Mudir and local officials were entertained.

The strength of the Battalion at the close of the year was, in Damanhour (exclusive of the Guides Company), 7 British and 9 Indian officers, 540 other ranks, 36 drivers, 46 followers and 83 mules. At Sidi Bisher, 1 British and 3 Indian officers, 166 other ranks, 3 drivers, 10 followers and 12 mules.

On 24 January 1920 a warning order to embark for India was received. This was confirmed on 27th instant when definite orders were given to entrain on 29th instant. On 29 January a company of the 2nd Battalion 56th Punjabi Rifles F.P. arrived, and these in conjunction with the company of the Guides already at Damanhour, took over all duties.

The same evening a troop train arrived which had brought C and D companies from Sidi Bisher, and in which the rest of the Battalion was entrained.

On 30 January the Battalion arrived at Suez docks and embarked on the transport *Franz Ferdinand* – its strength being 7 British and 12 Indian officers, 736 other ranks, 21 followers and 3 chargers.

The following British officers embarked: Lieut-Colonel A. G. Lind, D.S.O., Commanding; Captain A. I. G. McConkey; Captain R. G. Ekin; Captain E. M. Ashton: Lieutenant C. R. Spear; Lieutenant M. B. P. Reeve; Lieutenant T. L. Evans; two attached officers – Lieutenant F. P. Simons, 27th Cavalry and Lieutenant A. C. Maclaren 57th Rifles F.F. – had to be left in Egypt as reinforcement officers. Several complimentary orders were received on our departure from Egypt (two are noted in Appendix E).

The 47th Sikh Infantry embarked on the same transport, the whole being under command of Lieut-Colonel H. Boyce-Coombe, D.S.O., M.C., 47th Sikhs. More than 1,450 troops were on board and the ship was very crowded. No meat or milk ration was issued, but fortunately there was a large supply of milk remaining in the Battalion canteen which was much appreciated. The men were in high spirits at the thought of returning to India.

About 70 miles north of Perim Island we passed the steamship *Eriupura* piled up on a reef on to which she had run during a fog. On this ship five companies of the Battalion had embarked for France in September 1914. Later on she was cut into two parts and towed to Aden, where the parts were joined and the ship again made serviceable.

On 9 February 1920 the *Franz Ferdinand* arrived at Karachi and on 10th the Battalion disembarked, entrained at the docks and was taken to the rest camp being lodged in very much the same spot whereon it had camped five and a half years before when on its way to France. There were very few left who were able to remember that occasion.

On 13 February the Battalion entrained at Karachi and arrived at Multan on 14 February, and marched to the lines occupied by the Depot. The bands of the Buffs (East Kent Regiment) and the 14th Sikhs met the Battalion at the station, and marched with it to the lines.

The Depot gave its battalion a great reception and the next two days were given over to feasting and *tomasha*. Much had now to be done. The Depot had to be absorbed into the active battalion; men despatched on leave and furlo, field accounts settled, and men of other units returned to their own depots.

On 20 and 21 February, 31 other ranks of the 35th Rifles F.F. and 1 Indian officer and ranks of the 57th Rifles F.F. were sent away.

It was known that a considerable number of rewards in the form of grants of land and *Jangi Inams* (a monthly cash allowance lasting over two generations) were to be given, and the problem of deciding on the most deserving at last now confronted the Commanding Officer. Five hundred names came up for careful consideration, comprising Indian officers and men who had served throughout the war with the Battalion, others (as the Afridis and Yusufzais) who had served with other units for portions of the war, others who had done splendid work at the Depot, others who having been severely wounded or otherwise incapacitated had gone on pension, some, the heirs of those who had lost their lives in the war.

A system of marking was adopted in which the point taken most into consideration was actual service in the field, since it was laid down that the grants were made for service in the Great War. The pecuniary circumstances of Indian officers and men were also considered and some of those who were already well-provided with land and property and who had received decorations for service, were passed over by others equally deserving but whose need of land or money was greater. The number of grants made by Government was calculated on the number of casualties

Appendix A
Casualties

British Officers Killed

Lieut-Colonel W. E. Venour, killed in action	October 31 1914
Captain W. McM. Black, killed in action	October 31 1914
Lieut J. McA. Craig, 57th Rifles, F.F. (attached) killed in action	October 31 1914
Captain H. L. C. Baldwin, killed in action	November 23 1914
Lieut L. Gaisford, killed in action	November 23 1914
Lieut R. A. Reilly, 31st Punjabis (attached) killed in action	November 23 1914
Captain M. A. R. Bell, 54th Sikhs, F.F. (attached) killed in action	Dec, 20 1914
Captain C. H. Eliot, killed in action	April 27 1915
Lieut S. A. McMillan, I.A.R.O., died of wounds received in action	May 9 1915
Captain F.F. Hodgson, 84th Punjabis (attached) died of wounds received in action	May 17 1915
Lieut-Colonel C. E. D. Davidson-Houston, D.S.O., killed in action	September 25 1915
Captain J. H. Milligan, killed in action	September 25 1915
Lieut J. O. Nicolls, killed in action	September 25 1915
Captain A. Flagg, I.A.R.O. (attached) killed in action	September 25 1913
Captain K. B. Mackenzie, 123rd Rifles (attached) killed in action	September 25 1913
2nd Lieut F. B. Deane-Spread, I.A.R.O. (attached) killed in action	September 25 1915
Captain R. B. Kitson, killed in action	November 13 1917
Lieut B. Douglas, 101st Grenadiers (attached) killed in action	November 13 1917
Captain D. R. Montford, 98th Infantry (attached) missing, believed died of wounds received in action	March 30 1918

Lieut J. Mackay, I.A.R.O. (attached) killed in action — March 30 1918

British Officers Wounded

Captain A. G. Lind	November 23 1914
Captain E.S. C. Willis, D.S.O.	November 23 1914
Captain C. H. Elliot	December 10, 1914
Captain C. G. V. M. Wardell, 21st Punjabis (attached)	March 11 1915
Captain E. Grose, 16th Rajputs (attached)	March 11 1915
Captain A. A. Smith	March 12 1915
Captain J. Y. Tancred, 19th Punjabis, (attached)	April 25 1915
Captain G, S, Bull	May 9 1915
Major A. G. Thomson	May 9 1915
Lieut J. H. Milligan	July 5 1915
Captain C. B. Harcourt, 28th Punjabis (attached) wounded and captured	September 25 1915
Captain C. G. V. M. Wardell, 21st Punjabis (attached)	September 25 1915
Major R. de W. Waller	November 19 1917
Lieut S. T. Gray, I.A.R.O. (attached)	April 10 1918
2nd Lieut A. H. C. Allen, 2nd Battalion 4th Devon Regiment (attached)	September 19 1918

Indian Officers Killed

Subadar Wazir Singh, killed in action	November 23 1914
Jemadar Mardan Ali, killed in action	December 20 1914
Subadar Phuman Singh, I.D.S.M., died of wounds	February 13 1915
Subadar Bostan Khan, 82nd Punjabis (attached) killed in action	May 9 1915
Jemadar Lal Khan (attached) killed in action	May 9 1915
Jemadar Rakhmat, killed in action	May 17 1915
Subadar Sohel Singh, I.O.M., killed in action	September 25 1915
Jemadar Yar Dil, killed in action	September 25 1913
Jemadar Din Mohommad, 123rd Rifles (attached) killed in action	September 25 1913
Jemadar Fazal Dad, I.D.S.M., killed in action	November 1 1917
Subadar Lal Khan, I.O.M., killed	March 30 1918

Indian Officers Wounded

Subadar Khan Buhadur	October 31 1914
Subadar Abdul Ali	October 31 1914
Jemadar Sohel Singh	November 15 1914
Subadar Saiyid Gul	November 22 1914
Subadar Abdul Ali, Bahadur (2nd time)	November 23 1914
Subadar Gujar Singh	February 6 1915
Subadar Phuman Singh, I.D.S.M.	March 6 1915
Subadar Indar Singh, M.C., I.D.S.M.	March 9 1915
Subadar Karam Singh, I.O.M.	May 9 1915
Jemadar Hira Singh	May 9 1915
Jemadar Kehr Singh	May 9 1915
Jemadar Abdul Rahman	May 9 1915
Jemadar Hawinda, M.C., I.D.S.M.	May 9 1915
Subadar Hamid Khan, I.D.S.M.	May 17 1915
Jemadar Mir Zaman, 66th Punjabis (attached)	May 17 1915

Jemadar Mohommad Arabi, I.O.M.	May 18 1915
Jemadar Yar Dil	May 18 1915
Jemadar Huknat	June 4 1915
Jemadar Hamesh Gul	June 4 1915
Jemadar Yar Dil (2nd time)	July 11 1915
Subadar Raj Talab Babadur, I.D.S.M.	August 6 1915
Subadar Lal Singh	September 16 1915
Subadar Karam Dad, 123rd Rifles (Outrams)	September 25 1915
Jemadar Golodu, 54th Sikhs F.F.	October 9 1915
Subadar Shah Sowar, 101st Grenadiers (attached)	November 13 1917
Jemadar Hussein Bux, 101st Grenadiers (attached)	November 13 1917
Subadar Ahmad Din, 101st Grenadiers (attached)	November 13 1917
Subadar Karan Singh, I.O.M. (2nd time)	November 14 1917
Jemadar Mirza Khan	March 30 1918
Subalar Mohommad Arabi, I.O.M. (2nd time)	September 19 1918

Indian Other Ranks

Killed	288	Approximately 70 percent of these were exclusively 58th Rifles, the remainder being men of other units attached.
Died of Wounds	61	
Died of Sickness	46	Approximately 62 percent of these as above.
Wounded	1163	

Total Casualties

	British Officers	Indian Officers	Other Ranks
Killed	18	10	288
Died of wounds	2	1	61
Died of sickness	1	0	46
Wounded, missing and prisoners of war	15	30	1163
Total casualties	36	41	1558

Appendix B
List of Honours and Awards Gained by the Officers and Men of the 58th Rifles F.F., During The Great War 1914–18.

Distinguished Service Order

Lieut-Colonel C. E. D. Davidson-Houston	France 1914
Major A. G. Thomson	France 1915
Captain S. B. Pope	France 1915
Major A. G. Lind	Palestine 1917
Major R. de W. Waller	Palestine 1918

Military Cross

Captain G. S. Bull	France 1914
Jemadar Indar Singh, I.D.S.M.	France 1914
Jemadar Hawindah	France 1915
Captain S. Gordon, I.M.S.	France 1915
Captain G. R. Dowland	Palestine 1917
Lieut G. G. Hills	Palestine 1918

Indian Order of Merit First Class

Subadar Sohel Singh	France 1915
Subadar Mohommad Arabi Khan	Palestine 1917

Indian Order of Merit Second Class

Jemadar Sohel Singh	France 1914
Jemadar Harchand Singh	France 1914
No. 1811 Havildar Karam Singh	France 1914
No. 1848 Havildar Roshan Khan	France 1914
No. 3572 Havildar Saidak	France 1914
No. 3032 Havildar Lal Badshall	France 1914

No. 2823 Lance-Naik Sher Khan	France 1914
No. 2742 Sepoy Ishar Singh	France 1914
Jemadar Mohommad Arabi Khan	France 1915
No, 1925 Havildar Santa Singh	France 1915
No. 2830 Havildar Kashmir Singh	France 1915
No. 3131 Lance-Naik Phagan Singh	France 1915
Jemadar Diwana	Palestine 1918

Order of British India Second Class

Subadar Abdul Ali	France 1914
Subadar Raj Talab Khan	France 1915
Subadar-Major Tikka Khan	Palestine 1917–18
Subadar Gujar Singh	Indian Frontier 1917–18

Indian Distinguished Service Medal

Jemadar Hamid Khan	France 1914
Jemadar Indar Singh M.C.	France 1914
No. 3404 Naik Baidullah	France 1914
No. 2164 Havildar Sundar Singh	France 1914
No, 2512 Havildar Lashkarai	France 1914
Jemadar Mir Mast*	France 1914
Subadar Raj Talalb Khan	France 1914
No. 2763 Havildar Ajun Khan	France 1914
No. 3136 Havildar Sarfaraz	France 1914
No. 2758 Naik Dewa Singh	France 1914
No. 2634 Naik Zarghun Shah	France 1914
No. 3097 Sepoy Azam Khan*	France l914
No. 3133 Sepoy Maluk Singh	France 1914
No. 3374 Sepoy Dewa Singh (bar in 1917)	France 1914
No. 3080 Naik Zar Baz	France 1914
Jemadar Hawindah	France 1914
No. 3567 Lance-Naik Saiyid Asghar	France 1914
Subadar Phuman Singh	France 1915
No. 2198 Havildar Fazl Dad	France 1915

No. 3066 Naik Sardar Khan	France 1915
No. 2934 Sepoy Mohammad Amin	France 1915
No. 3323 Havildar Fazl Dad	Palestine 1917
No. 3835 Lance-Naik Rahim Ali	Palestine 1917
No. 3374 Naik Dewa Singh I.D.S.M. (bar)	Palestine 1917
No, 2927 Lance-Naik Bhag Singh	Palestine 1917
No. 2841 Naik Wadhawa	Palestine 1918
No. 3291 Sepoy Kapura	Palestine 1918
No. 4341 Sepoy Jaimal Singh	Palestine 1918
No. 4141I Sepoy Damodar	Palestine 1918
No. 3704 Lance-Naik Diwan Singh	Palestine 1918
No. 4778 Sepoy Bhola Singh	Palestine 1918
No. 2938 Lance-Naik Pritam Sing	Palestine 1918
No. 651 Sepoy Fuiru	Palestine 1918
No. 4263 Sepoy Bara Singh	Palestine 1918
No. 4387 Sepoy Amar Singh	Palestine 1918
No. 4707 Sepoy Hakim Singh	Palestine 1918

* Afterwards deprived of their decoration for desertion

Foreign Decorations Awarded

Russian
Order of St Stanislaus Third Class.
Lieut-Colonel E. R. B. Murray

Cross of St George Fourth Class
No. 3080 Niak Zar Baz

Serbian
Order of the White Eagle Fifth Class
Subadar Tikka Khan

Silver Star
No. 3722 Naik Redi Gul

Gold Medal
No. 3457 Naik Safirullah

French
Croix de Guerre.
Major A. G. Lind.

The following decorations were gained by officers and men of other units while serving with the 58th Rifles F.F.

Military Cross

2nd Lieut A. H. C. Allen, 2nd Battalion 4th Devonshire Regiment	Palestine 1918

Indian Order of Merit Second Class.

Subadar Lal Khan, 55th Rifles, F.F.	Palestine 1918

Indian Distinguished Service Medal.

Subadar Ahmad Din, 1/101st Grenadiers	Palestine 1917
No. 1873 Naik Mohommad Yusuf, 1/101st Grenadiers	Palestine 1917
No 1893 Sepoy Mohommad Khan, 1/101st Grenadiers	Palestine 1917
No. 1177 Lance-Naik Gaur Ali, 1/101st Grenadiers	Palestine 1917
No. 1226 Sepoy Umar Khan, 1/101st Grenadiers	Palestine 1917
No. 1968 Sepoy Dilbar Shah, 1/101st Grenadiers	Palestine 1917
No. 4000 Sepoy Mohommad Khan, 2/101st Grenadiers	Palestine 1917

Special Rewards for Service in The Great War

Jagirs of land.

Subadar Mohommad Arabi Khan
Subadar-Major and Honorary Captain Mir Alam Khan, Sirlar Bahadar

Special Assignment of Land Revenue

Subadar Indar Singh, M.C., I.D.S.M.

Grants of land.

104 of which 19 were assigned to Indian officers, who each received two squares and 66 to Indian other ranks.

Jungi Inam.

84 of which 2 to Indian officers and 82 to Indian other ranks,

Appendix C
List of Units from Which Reinforcements were Received

Date	Unit	B.O.	I.O.	O.R
December 1914	91st Punjabis*	1	2	204
12–2–1915	82nd Punjabis	1	3	97
1–4–1915	82nd Punjabis		1	31
1–4–1915	54th Sikhs, F.F.		1	62
12–5–1915	82nd Punjabis			49
12–5–1915	66th Punjabis			11
18–6–1915	76th Punjabis			26
26–8–1915	123rd Outram's Rifles	2	4	162
5–3–1916	55th Rifles, F.F.		1	138
9–2–1917	55th Rifles, F.F.	1	6	218
24–10–1917	101st Grenadiers	1	4	208
18–12–1917	101st Grenadiers	1	2	74
21–3–1918	98th Infantry	2	3	205
18–10–1918	57th Rifles, F.F.	1		74
9–12–1918	57th Rifles, F.F.		2	110
Total Reinforcements		10	29	1669

*This draft was composed of Dogras and was re-transferred after a few days to the 39th Garhwal Rifles.

The Battalion was thus reinforced by representatives of ten different Units

In addition to the above 1,661 Indian officers and men were despatched as reinforcements from the Battalion Depot in India to the Battalion in the field, most of these were enlisted and trained at the Depot in India. The remainder being either Battalion reservists or trained men of the Battalion left in India in September 1914.

Appendix D
Recruits Enlisted at the Depot
Between August 1914 and November 1918

Sikhs	715
Punjabi Mohammadans	1493
Dogras	250
Yusufzais	377
Yusufzais	90
Total	2925

In addition to the above, 426 Multanis were enlisted and trained at the Battalion Depot; these were transferred to the 2nd Battalion 56th Rifles F.F. when that unit was formed at Multan in July 1917.

Appendix E
Extracts From Orders and Letters

I   Letter from Lt Gen. Sir J. Willcocks, 10 November 1914

II   Extract from an Order of the Day by Lt Gen. Sir J. Willcocks, 7 December 1914

III   Special Order of the Day by Field Marshal Sir J. French, 22 November 1915

IV   Message from H. M. The King-Emperor to the I. A. Corps in France, December 1915

V   Letter from Lt Colonel A. G. Wauchope, Commanding 2nd Bn, The Black Watch, December 1915

VI   Message from XXI Corps, 23 November 1917

VII   Extract from message issued by Major Gen P. C. Palin, 9 January 1918

VIII   Message from 234 Brigade, 18 March 1918

IX   Special Order of the Day by Gen. Sir E. H. H. Allenby, 26 September 1918

X   Message from Major Gen. P. C. Palin, 2 March 1919

XI   Letter from Major Gen. G. F. Gorringe, 21 January 1920

XII   Letter from Field Marshal Lord Allenby, 27 January 1920

I

Letter from Lieut-General Sir J. Willcocks.
HEADQUARTERS I. A. CORPS
Dated 10–11–1914.

To,
O. C. 58th Rifles F.F.
I much deplore your heavy losses but I am confident you will maintain and add to the good name of the Frontier Force.

Please convey my best wishes to all ranks.

(Sd) James Willcocks,
L.G., I. A. Corps

II Extract

Indian Army Corps.
Order of the Day
By
Lieut-Genl Sir James Willcocks, K.C.B., K.C.S.I., K.C.M.G.
D.S.O. Commander.
Dated 7th December 1914

Now that the reports of the action on 23rd and 24th November east of Festubert are all to hand, the Corps Commander has learnt with great satisfaction of the conduct of the troops engaged under Brig.-General Egerton, C.B.

*****

A considerable number of the troops of both divisions were engaged, and under the circumstances it is difficult to single out corps, but the steadiness of the Black Watch and the portion of the 58th Rifles next to them, and especially the flank attack by the 1st Battalion 39th Garhwal Rifles, which helped to regain the lost trenches, merit special notice.

*****

The Corps Commander will have great pleasure in bringing the names of units and individual officers and other ranks specially deserving to the notice of the Field Marshal Commanding in Chief.

                    (Sd.) W. E. O'Leary, Brigadier-General
                    Deputy Adjutant ad Quartermaster General

III

Special Order of the Day
by
Field Marshal Sir J. D. P. French, G.C.B., O.M., G.C.V.O., K.C.M.G.
Commander-in-Chief, British Army in the Field.

On the departure of the Indian Corps from my command, under which you have fought for more than a year, I wish to send a message of thanks to all officers, non-commissioned officers and men for the work you have done for the Empire.

From the time you reached France you were constantly engaged with the enemy until the end of last year. After a few weeks rest you returned to the trenches and since then you have continually held some portion of the front line, taking part in the important and successful engagements of Neuve Chapelle, and of Richebourge, and in the heavy fighting at the end of September. The Lahore Division was also engaged in the severe actions near Ypres in April and May.

That your work has been hard is proved by the number of your casualties.

The British troops of the Corps have borne themselves in a manner worthy of the best traditions of the Army.

The Indian troops have also shown most praiseworthy courage under novel and trying conditions, both of climate and of fighting, and have not only upheld, but added to, the good name of the Army which they represent.

This is all the more praiseworthy in view of the heavy losses among British officers having deprived the Indian ranks of many trusted leaders whom they knew well, and of the fact that the drafts necessary to maintain your strength have frequently had to be drawn from regiments quite unconnected with the units they were sent to reinforce.

You have done your work here well, and are now being another place where an unscrupulous enemy has stirred up strife against the King-Emperor.

I send you all my good wishes for success in the part you will now be called on to play in this great war, I thank you for the services you have rendered while under my command, and trust that the united efforts of the Allies may soon bring the enemy to his knees and restore peace to the world.

                                (sd) J. D. P. French, Field Marshal,
                                Commanding-in-Chief, the British
22nd November, 1915   Army in the Field

IV
Message of His Majesty The King-Emperor to the British and Indian troops of the Indian Army Corps in France.

Officers, Non-Commissioned Officers, and men of the Indian Army.

More than a year ago I summoned you from India to fight for the safety of My Empire and the honour of my pledged word on the battlefields of Belgium and France. The confidence which I then expressed in your senses of duty, your courage and your chivalry, you have since then nobly justified.

I now require your services in another field of action: but before you leave France I send my dear and gallant son, the Prince of Wales, who has shared with my Armies the dangers and hardships of the campaign, to thank you in my name for your services and to express to you my satisfaction.

British and Indian comrades-in-arms, yours has been a fellowship in toils and hardships, in courage and endurance often against great odds, in deeds nobly done in days of ever-memorable conflict. In a warfare waged under new conditions and in peculiarly trying circumstances, you have worthily upheld the honour of the Empire and the great traditions of my Army in India.

I have followed your fortunes with the deepest interest and watched your gallant actions with pride and satisfaction; I mourn with you the loss of many gallant officers and men. Let it be your consolation, as it was their pride, that they freely gave their lives in a just cause for the honour of their Sovereign and the safety of My Empire. They died as gallant soldiers, and I shall ever hold their sacrifice in grateful remembrance.

You leave France with a just pride in honourable deeds already achieved and with my assured confidence that your proved valour and experience will contribute to further victories in the new fields of action to which you go.

I pray God to bless and guard you and to bring you back safely, when the final victory is won, each to his own home – there to be welcomed with honour among his own people.

V
Copy of a Letter Received
from
Lt Colonel A. G. Wauchope, C.M.G., D.S.O.,
Comdg 2 / Black Watch

Dear Colonel Murray,

I hear today that your Regiment is not coming further East, and that the Black Watch and 58th are therefore to be separated after serving side by side for over a year.

I speak on behalf of the Regiment when I say that we all regret that we cannot go on fighting together in the new campaign as we have for so long, in good times and in evil, in France.

But with regrets there are other feelings that come to my mind on parting; there are memories that you and I may forget, but that will ever be fresh in the history of the two regiments: memories of November 23rd when together we drove the Germans out of the line, and chased them back from their own sapheads; memories of many nights when I and other officers have gone scouting out ahead with men of your regiment, and memories above all of September 25th, when Colonel Davidson-Houston, like the gallant soldier he was, brought your regiment forward from the second line to protect the exposed flank of the Black Watch, and a fine sight it was to see the 58th pushing forward driving everything before them, and it cheered our men too, for a years experience had taught them that there was no regiment who ever served in the Bareilly Brigade they'd as soon have as the 58th to come to their aid: indeed they'd rather the 58th above all others.

I write in haste Colonel but I write with such feeling I cannot write with clearness: so many have gone who were old and trusted friends, from Venour to many others, but you will remember me to Gordon and to those Native officers with some of whom I have fought in attack and in reconnaissance, whose names have mostly gone from me but the memory of whose courage and devotion can never die.

Believe me
Yours very sincerely
December 1915

A. G. Wauchope Lt Col
Comdg 2/ Black Watch

VI
Message from XXI Corps
To,
58th Riles.
No. BM 1002   Date 24th November 1917

Following wire has been received from 21st Corps:
75th Division
CH 146   23/11

Following from C. G. S. begins AAA Chief congratulates 5th Mounted Bde, 52 and 75 Divns on their achievement AAA They have driven a stubborn enemy from position after position in a rugged country where everything favoured him AAA The tactical leading has been of the first order and reflects the greatest credit on all troops referred to AAA
Ends.

From 234 Bde
(Sd) C. E. Graham Captain

VII
Extract from message from Major-General P. C. Palin.

I wish to convey in writing to all ranks my appreciation of the excellent work performed by the 75th Division from the day when it marched out of the Sheikh Abbas Salient in pursuit of the Turk. I have already expressed my opinion verbally to G. Os. C. Brigades and Os. C. battalions but I wish it to be known to all ranks of the Division.

The capture of Junction Station and Latron, the forcing of the strong positions astride the Jerusalem Road leading to Enab, the relentless pursuit of the Turk culminating in the fighting which secured and retained Neby Samwel in the face of numerically superior artillery, are all feats of which any Division may well be proud.

Bad weather and reduced rations, brought up with great difficulty, rendered the success achieved by men in their summer clothing still more

110-R	(Sd) P. C. Palin, Major-General,
D/15/1/18	Commanding 75th Division
9th January, 1918	

VIII
Copy of 75th Divisional Letter A.Q. 202|16, dated 15–3–18

On behalf of the Divisional Artillery, I wish to thank the R. E. and Infantry who have been engaged in making the roads which enabled us to advance our guns while operations were in progress, in a difficult country.

Officers and men alike recognise the amount of work involved, and are grateful accordingly.
Copy to,
58th Rifles
496 Coy R. E.

Forwarded
The Major-General Commanding the Division wishes it to be known that it was only by the strenuous work put in by the Engineers and Infantry that it was possible to move up the guns to cooperate. I am also directed to state that the B.G.C. wishes to thank you personally for the invaluable work you have done in making roads for guns and supplies during the recent operations.
(Sd.) A. Saunders, Captain,
Staff Captain
Dated 18–3–18   234 Inf. Bde

IX
Special order of the day, 26th September 1918

I desire to convey to all ranks and all arms of the Force under my command, my admiration and thanks for their great deeds of the past week, and my appreciation of their gallantry and determination which have resulted in the total destruction of the VIIth and VIIIth Turkish Armies opposed to us.

Such a complete Victory has seldom been known in all the history of war

26th Sept: 1918 (Sd) E. H. H. Allenby, General, C in C

X
Message from Major-General P. O. Palin

Before any more units leave the Division and before further Demobilisation takes place, I wish to thank you all, Commanders, staffs and all ranks for what you have done and for the loyal support you have always given me.

The 75th Division was formed a little over a year and seven months ago. The period is not long, but has been quite long enough for the Division to make a name for itself and to create the splendid reputation which it now holds. The successful raids on the old British trenches, Outpost Hill and Middlesex Hill, the break out from Gaza, the rapid advance to Junction Station and thence, driving the Turks before it through Bab el Wad, the capture of Nebi Sanmwel, the key to Jerusalem; such is the record of the 75th Division for the first six months of its existence. A few weeks later the Division captured the line Kibbeah – Kh.Ibannelh – Horse Shoe, followed shortly by the five mile jump to Berukin – El Kefr – Deir Ballut – Umn Tawaky, and finally, after a few months of wearisome trench warfare, the monotony of which was somewhat lessened by occasional raids, the Division took part in one of the greatest and most successful operations of the War – the total defeat of the Turk and the capture of Palestine. This is a magnificent record and one of which the 75th Division may be justly proud. It has been attained by courage, good discipline and a fine spirit of comradeship and unselfishness qualities which go to make the finest soldiers. It is such men whom I have had the privilege and good fortune to command.

As we shall soon be separated and scattered to different parts of the world, I take the opportunity of wishing everyone who is present with the Division and those who have already left it, a joyful reunion on their return to their homes and the best of luck and happiness in the future.

Hdqrs. 73th Div.   (Sd) P. C. Palin, Major-General,
2nd March 1919.   Commanding 75th Division

XI
Letter from Major-General G. F. Gorringe.

                      HEADQUARTERS, 10TH DIVISION
Officer Commanding,   X.G./M/332
  58th Rifles   21st January, 1920

On your leaving the 10th Division on your return to India, I desire to place on record my very high appreciation of the efficiency of the Battalion and the excellent work which it has at all times carried out while under my command. You have been called on to carry out many varied and onerous duties in maintaining order in Egypt, you have always responded to these Calls in a most loyal and devoted manner.

You have set a good example as soldiers, your discipline has been excellent, your turn out and smartness on parade and when on Guard has been most creditable thank you all sincerely and especially you Colonel Lind for your loyal devotion to duty and the help you have given me at all times.

I wish you all a pleasant voyage back to India and all success in the future.
(Sd) G. F. Gorringe, Major-General
Commanding 10th Division

XII
Letter from Field Marshal Lord Allenby.
Officer Commanding,
58th Rifles.

On your departure from Egypt and the Egyptian Expeditionary Force, please express to all ranks my high appreciation of the services they have rendered, and their admirable spirit and conduct in all circumstances.

Your Battalion has worthily upheld the fighting traditions of the Indian Army.

I thank you and wish you a safe return to India.
(Sd) Allenby, Field Marshal,
G.H.Q., E.E.F.   Commander-in-Chief.
27th January, 1920   Egyptian Expeditionary Force

OTHER BOOKS FROM GOSLING PRESS

Operations of the Mounted Troops of the Egyptian Expeditionary Force
By W J Foster, J G Browne and Rex Osborne

The E.E.F. came into being in March 1916 from the remnants of the British troops from Gallipoli and the troops already in Egypt although it lost ten of its fourteen infantry divisions to other theatres in quick order. The multinational force of Australians, New Zealanders, Indians and British Territorial troops became a strategic reserve for the British Army

This fascinating book was originally published as a series of ten articles in the Cavalry Journal between 1921 and 1923. The articles were an attempt to bring together learning form what was probably the last major cavalry campaign.

Regimental History of the 1st Battalion 8th Punjab Regiment
by N M Geoghegan and M H.A. Campbell

The 89th Punjabis had a most distinguished record of service during the First World War. They have the unique distinction of claiming to have served in more theatres of war than any other unit of the British Empire in that conflict. These included: Aden (Yemen), Egypt, Gallipoli, France, Mesopotamia, North West Frontier of India, Salonika (Greece), and the Russian Transcaucasia, where they served from 1918-20 as part of the British Expeditionary Force.

All Gosling Press book are available direct from www.goslingpress.co.uk or from Amazon

www.ingramcontent.com/pod-product-compliance
Lightning Source LLC
Chambersburg PA
CBHW072054110526
44590CB00018B/3171